Bill Mueller's engaging and entertainin
large family show us the charm and c
largely unknown today. Enjoy the stories

MW00904038

Racine, Wisconsin
Retired High School Principal, Local Government Leader

The book should provide a blueprint for parents who wish to build a family, but it also describes life in rural Midwestern United States. As an only child, I found it very interesting. The farming brought back memories, some from even before Bill's time. I hope the book gets the attention it deserves. I certainly recommend it. With all the time given to their family, his parents lived to ages far beyond average. His parents were devoted Catholics who taught their children to work hard and live by The Golden Rule.

—Jack Marlowe
Maquoketa, Iowa
Iowa Newspaper Association Distinguished Service Award Winner
Iowa High School Athletic Association Media Award Winner
Maquoketa Community High School Friend of Education Award Winner

---

Growing up as an Iowa farm boy myself in the 1960s, I can appreciate the storyline behind *Time to Ship Another Steer.* The book brings back memories of our old barn, house, winters, and the jobs we had to do. An enjoyable read. Thanks, Bill, for writing your story that we all can relate to.

—Leighton Hepker
43 years at KMAQ Radio, Maquoketa, Iowa

Time to Ship Another Steer is a living history book as seen and experienced by Bill. Anyone with family or friends involved in farming in the last 75 years will enjoy this book. Progress in farming has separated many of us from our heritage. *Time to Ship Another Steer* will take you back to those days and to appreciate the current times.

—Bob Thiel
DeWitt, Iowa
Retired educator and business owner

Bill Mueller's first published book shared his trials and tribulations while teaching driver education. Now he has written a new publication that recalls memories of growing up on a farm with ten siblings. Bill's latest release, describing his early life, reveals many amusing and amazing personal tales to provide both interesting and enjoyable reading.

—Bill Homrighausen
DeWitt, Iowa
Author, *They Call Me Mr. DeWitt,* Community Benefactor and Booster

---

Not having grown up in a farming family, I had no idea what the family had to perform before coming to school and after they got home. They appeared each day smiling, neat, and tidy, ready to meet the day's expectations. The boys became altar boys, learning all the responses in Latin. They were a delightful group, and you could always count on them.

—Andrea (Aiello) Malsch
Bill, Mark, Jane, & Steve's sixth-grade teacher, revered by the children's mother, Marcella
Buyer for Snap-On Tools and Milwaukee Electric Tool: Racine, Wisconsin

Time to Ship Another Steer

Bill Mueller

Mueller
Times

Media

ISBN: 9781986159777

Mueller
Times

Media

Preface

It has been a fun ride these past two years since my first book, *Come Drive With Me!* was published. Chasing a dream has been rewarding, people's feedback exciting, and the new friendships special. Many people have asked, "When is your second driving book coming out?" *Come Drive With Me II* is in the works, but it is not my next endeavor.

Instead, I decided to give you a peek into what farm living was like for me, and the blessing it was growing up in a large family. I shared with Christine Gilroy, my editor, that I was writing a collection of memories growing up on the farm as one of eleven children. She loved the idea. I told her that when money was tight and a bill had to be paid, Dad would ship another steer to cover the bill. The title, *Time to Ship Another Steer*, better demonstrates the theme I was striving to convey, which was Mom and Dad's love for each other, their children, and everyone they knew.

Though you can't go back in time, country life is still available for all who have a dream to live so. Recently my wife, Audrey, and I each met people who moved from the city in the past year. They both wanted to live at a slower pace with less stress and fewer traffic lights. To them, recreational opportunities were closer, schools smaller, and friendships easier to make in the country.

I knew to make this work error-free, my brothers and sisters had to see it. I sent them the rough draft, even before Audrey or Christine had a chance to fix my spelling, punctuation, and homonyms. Though scary, it was the quickest way to get *Time To Ship Another Steer* to press.

Sometimes I use the terms choleric, sanguine, melancholy, and phlegmatic. These are the personality temperaments first explained by the ancient Greek physician Hippocrates in 400 B.C. A choleric person is a take-charge person, sanguine a life of the party, melancholy a detail person, and phlegmatic an easy-going person. Author Florence Littauer writes extensively on these temperaments. Her hilarious book *Personality Plus* will give any reader a great understanding of why people behave as they do.

Acknowledgments

I thank God for my opportunities and His blessings.

I would like to thank my wife, Audrey, for her love, patience, support, and creativity these past 45 years. Audrey created all drawings in the book and placed photos for the book. I appreciate her ability to visualize, as well as the talent she has to put these fun images on paper. Audrey, once again thank you for helping me bring my stories to life.

Mom and Dad were extraordinary. I hope everyone who reads this book will get a glimpse of how special they were to all who knew them. They were raised during the Depression. Materially, their families didn't have much more than the land they lived on, but what they did have were hardworking, honest, loving parents. Mom and Dad in turn passed on those lessons to all eleven of us kids. The two Bible verses that best exemplify Mom and Dad's lives would be The Golden Rule: Do Unto Others as You Would Have Them Do Unto You (Luke 6:31). The second was, To Whom Much Is Given, Much Is Required (Luke 12:48).

The love and support of Mom and Dad, my siblings, aunts, uncles, neighbors, and friends made this book possible.

I am blessed to have such a loving and supportive family: Tom; Mike and his wife, Vernay; Mary and her husband, Mark Reinhart; Ellen and her husband, Emil Pfenninger; Mark and his wife, Barbara; Jane Powell; Steve; Tim and his wife, Sally; Donna and her husband, Ben Wilson; and Beth and her husband, John Schumacher.

Tom, thanks for your input. If I go to my grave being remembered as a respectable raconteur, my journey will be complete. Mary, helping me eliminate my glaring errors has been invaluable. Steve and Beth, I am grateful for all the time you spent proofing my work. I would never have been able to get everyone's name spelled correctly. You made my deadline easier to reach.

Thanks to my children and their families — Whitney and her husband, Bob Jost; Tyler and his wife, Samantha; Marcy and her husband, David McElroy — for the encouragement and continual technical support you give me to survive in the 21st century!

I believe God sent Christine Gilroy to me to edit my work and to lead Audrey and me through the maze of details necessary to make both of my books a reality. Christine has been a gold mine of knowledge and support for DeWitt and surrounding community authors. Not only has Christine helped aspiring authors complete their books, she has been instrumental in spotlighting our local talent.

I appreciate all the readers who kindly supported *Come Drive With Me.*

I thank Merlyn Usher, now gone, my friend, coach, and guide for more than thirty years.

I thank John McLean, "Uncle John" to my kids. He has been a brother for four decades.

Special Thanks

I want to thank Bob Johansen's children for supporting my decision to feature their father's painting on the cover of *Time To Ship Another Steer*. They include Christine Hoffman, John, my classmate Ann Worden, Roberta Gray, Larry, and Paul.

The award-winning artist Bob Johansen was once recognized as the top watercolor artist in the state of Wisconsin. Though he was best known for his lighthouse paintings, his daughter Ann said her father's most treasured "Johansen Originals" were his children. He became good friends with Mom and Dad, frequently painting our family's farm, sometimes even teaching classes on site. Most of Bob's paintings of the farm were winter scenes, with the exception of the spring scene Audrey and I chose to put on the cover of *Time To Ship Another Steer*. Over the years, Bob generously gave Mom and Dad fourteen original paintings.

Once while I was home visiting, Bob dropped off three or four paintings after his show season was finished that year. One was in a beautiful frame and sat proudly on display in Mom and Dad's living room for more than forty years. Each one of us was given one of his paintings for our wedding. Because of Bob's big heart, Mom and Dad were able to give each of us kids a priceless heirloom. Mom and Dad reciprocated as best they could with her hand-painted cookies and Christmas cards, and as many pies, fruits, vegetables, and flowers as he could ever use. All of us are forever grateful to him for his kindness.

Time to Ship Another Steer

Ship a steer is what Mom and Dad did when another bill had to be paid as they were raising eleven children.

This book is a collection of memories of growing up on the farm as one of those eleven children. Most people living today have no idea what farm life was like fifty years ago. Even kids who were lucky enough to have grown up farming weren't blessed with ten brothers and sisters and two iconic parents.

Audrey Mueller took this photo of her grandchildren Cece Jost and Gibson Jost. The calf is owned by Ron Seys.

I hope you love this book and share it with all your friends and family.

The Family of Edwin "Red" and Marcella Mueller

Back: Steve, Bill, Jane, Tom, Ellen, Mike, Mary, Mark.
Front: Marcella, Donna, Tim, Beth, Red.

Christmas 1969

Meet the Muellers

I thought if I introduced my brothers and sisters, my readers would enjoy *Time To Ship Another Steer* even more. Let me introduce them to you in their birth order.

Tom was a member of St. Catherine's forensic team. His senior year he won the conference four-minute speech contest and graduated one of the top competitors in the state of Wisconsin. He served in the U.S. Army, reaching the rank of Sergeant (E-5) while serving in Japan. For a time he taught in Wales, UK. When his late wife, Bonny, was diagnosed with Huntington's Disease he became active in the HD Family, serving six years on HDSA-Wisconsin Board of Directors. Tom is currently a partner with his son Dan in Eternal Image and Sound, a videography business in Oconomowoc.

Tom was the first to attend St. Norbert, then Mary, Ellen, Steve, and Beth. Mike went to University of Wisconsin-La Crosse and Gateway Community College. Mark, Jane, Tim, and Donna went to University of Wisconsin-Platteville. I went to Loras College in Dubuque, Iowa, to wrestle. I was excited about telling everybody I went to college out of state. Dubuque, Iowa, and Wisconsin are separated only by the Mississippi River.

In school, Mike was always Mr. Popularity. With his sanguine personality, he has always had a special talent for sharing his latest harrowing experience at work with a joke or two. He is one of the funniest people I have ever known.

Mary took four years of Latin in high school; her senior year she also took Russian. As part of a college exchange program, she lived nine months in Arequipa, Peru. After returning, she finished a major in Spanish and taught thirty-six years of high school Spanish. Mary is a passionate traveler, having visited much of the Western Hemisphere.

Ellen knitted black-and-white St. Catherine scarves for Mark and me when we were freshmen. Mine was a prized possession all through high school. I still have it. She made baby quilts for her children and many of her nieces and nephews. More recently, all of Mom and Dad's great-grandchildren have received a baby quilt, these alone numbering thirty-five. Ellen is my daughter Whitney's godmother, and she has made Whitney three quilts.

Mark is Mr. Stability. He owns Mueller's Tree and Sawmill Service. His business comes from word-of-mouth advertising. He has many faithful clients because of his attention to detail, and he's a Golden Rule practitioner.

Everyone agrees Jane is most like Mom. She is kind, with that same witty humor, and the ability to carry you along on her latest adventure. She was a teacher for more than thirty-five years. Jane volunteers at the Siena Center Convent, so she often has a nun story or two to share. Now that Mom is gone, Jane is probably our family's best Sheepshead player.

Steve has always been the information king of our family. In third grade he knew everything about each state. He knew the capital, the state bird, and countless details for them all. Whenever we kids had a trivia dispute, we consulted Steve before we went to the encyclopedia. Years later he appeared on the Jeopardy game show and won $15,000 in one episode. Steve is also an avid traveler who loves to explore geography, at home and abroad.

Tim is Mr. Fix-It. I don't think there is any type of household project he can't solve. He has been greatly appreciated by all of us for keeping Mom and Dad's c. 1850 farmhouse operational.

It was either Donna or Beth who said she spent many Friday evenings watching the road, looking forward to her older brothers and sisters coming home for the weekend or vacation. Because of our age difference, I missed much of their growing up. As a big brother, when I was visiting I should have spent more time with them. Regardless, I have been blessed to have them as my sisters. Donna and Beth were easy to raise, Mom always used to say. I guess God figured Mom had served her penance raising us boys.

It makes sense that both Ellen and Donna, like Dad, have a green thumb. Ellen graduated in biology, and Donna had an agriculture major. Donna enjoyed sports and the outdoors.

Donna and Beth have always been very close. Beth learned to read at four and loved playing school. She didn't have to talk much because Donna did it for her. Beth is the youngest. She was and still is the peacekeeper.

Pedigree Chart for
William Edwin Mueller

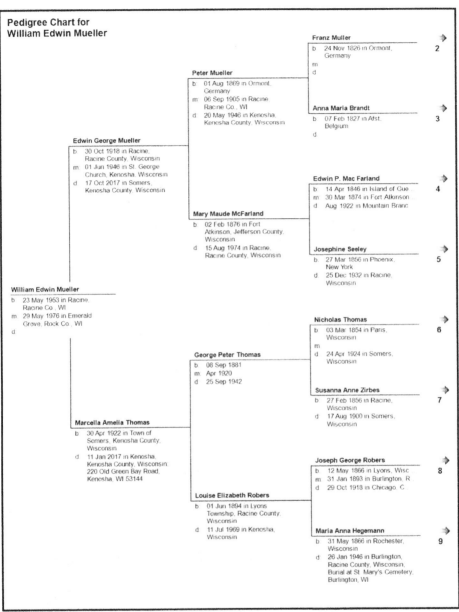

Franz Muller
b: 24 Nov 1826 in Ormont, Germany
m:
d:
→ 2

Peter Mueller
b: 01 Aug 1869 in Ormont, Germany
m: 06 Sep 1905 in Racine, Racine Co., WI
d: 20 May 1946 in Kenosha, Kenosha County, Wisconsin

Anna Maria Brandt
b: 07 Feb 1827 in Afst, Belgium
d:
→ 3

Edwin George Mueller
b: 30 Oct 1918 in Racine, Racine County, Wisconsin
m: 01 Jun 1946 in St. George Church, Kenosha, Wisconsin
d: 17 Oct 2017 in Somers, Kenosha County, Wisconsin

Edwin P. Mac Farland
b: 14 Apr 1846 in Island of Gue
m: 30 Mar 1874 in Fort Atkinson
d: Aug 1922 in Mountain Branc
→ 4

Mary Maude McFarland
b: 02 Feb 1876 in Fort Atkinson, Jefferson County, Wisconsin
d: 15 Aug 1974 in Racine, Racine County, Wisconsin

Josephine Seeley
b: 27 Mar 1856 in Phoenix, New York
d: 25 Dec 1932 in Racine, Wisconsin
→ 5

William Edwin Mueller
b: 23 May 1953 in Racine, Racine Co., WI
m: 29 May 1976 in Emerald Grove, Rock Co., WI
d:

Nicholas Thomas
b: 03 Mar 1854 in Paris, Wisconsin
m:
d: 24 Apr 1924 in Somers, Wisconsin
→ 6

George Peter Thomas
b: 08 Sep 1881
m: Apr 1920
d: 25 Sep 1942

Susanna Anne Zirbes
b: 27 Feb 1856 in Racine, Wisconsin
d: 17 Aug 1900 in Somers, Wisconsin
→ 7

Marcella Amelia Thomas
b: 30 Apr 1922 in Town of Somers, Kenosha County, Wisconsin
d: 11 Jan 2017 in Kenosha, Kenosha County, Wisconsin; 220 Old Green Bay Road, Kenosha, WI 53144

Joseph George Robers
b: 12 May 1866 in Lyons, Wisc
m: 31 Jan 1893 in Burlington, R
d: 29 Oct 1918 in Chicago, C
→ 8

Louise Elizabeth Robers
b: 01 Jun 1894 in Lyons Township, Racine County, Wisconsin
d: 11 Jul 1969 in Kenosha, Wisconsin

Maria Anna Hegemann
b: 31 May 1866 in Rochester, Wisconsin
d: 26 Jan 1946 in Burlington, Racine County, Wisconsin, Burial at St. Mary's Cemetery, Burlington, WI
→ 9

Red and
Marcella
Mueller

Chapter 1: A Little Background

My parents were at Dad's doctor appointment when he was in his eighties. The doctor scolded him for having so many children. She asked, "Why didn't you use birth control?" Mom answered her question with, "We did, that is why we only had eleven kids." I'm sure glad Mom and Dad followed God's plan, because the world is a much better place.

Mom prayed that all of us kids be born close in pairs, so as we grew we would always have a playmate. Mark and I were like twins. We were classmates from third grade on and almost inseparable.

Mark and I started college three hours from home on the same day. Mom and Dad dropped me off first at Loras College in Dubuque, Iowa, and then Mark at the University of Wisconsin-Platteville. It was an exciting time yet scary. Up to that time our whole life had revolved around the farm on which we grew up. It didn't take much to prepare for our departure. We just had to pack our clock radios and study lamps, and divide up our clothes the night before we left.

Mom's classroom of life's lessons had prepared each of us to meet the big world out there. For me, I found myself placed on the doorstep of Keane Hall where I would live the next four years being groomed for my life's journey. Three days later, I was terribly homesick. One of my dorm-mates, who happened also to be from Kenosha, was taking a load of guys to Platteville for a night on the town, where the drinking age was eighteen. I arrived at Mark's dorm room at 8 p.m. with instructions to be back on Second Street by 11 p.m. to catch my ride back to Dubuque. It was a weeknight and I wouldn't want to be late for Thursday morning classes. I didn't need to drink, I just wanted time to spend with Mark.

This was the first of many trips, many of which were by thumb, to and from Platteville to see Mark during our college years.

Growing up my family was so close, especially Mark and I. People thought we were twins because we were in the same grade in school. At ages five and six we agreed to stop calling each other Marky and Billy. We thought we were getting too old to be addressed with such childish names. About that same time we gave up crying for the same reason.

Mark and I have been through it all. The great outdoors, as well as the barn, was our playground. There was never a shortage of adventure for little boys to get into. Our work ethic was developed from the farm chores we did. Catholic schools gave us our thirst for knowledge, and holidays cemented our love for family and all who came to our door.

Mom and Dad Start a Family

Dad dated quite a bit as a young man. Before he left for Army boot camp in the fall of 1941, he had dated Mom just a few times. Dad's and her courtship was by mail, and Dad was a good letter writer.

While Dad was in the Army, Mom was that caring neighbor who gladly ran errands for Dad's mother. Neither of my grandmothers ever drove a car, so Mom used to come help Mary, Dad's mother, and they became very close. In one of Grandma's letters to Dad in the service, Grandma spoke highly of Mom: "You'd better not let this one get away."

When Dad got home from World War II in the summer of 1945 he and Mom got engaged, but she made him wait until the following spring to get married. On June 1, 2016, they celebrated their seventieth anniversary.

Tom was born in 1947, Mike in 1949, Mary in 1951, Ellen in 1952. I was born in 1953, Mark followed in 1954, and Jane was born in 1955. She was the first of the "three little kids." Steve was born in 1957, Tim in 1959. Donna came along in 1964, and Beth, the baby, was born in 1966. We were all born in boy or girl pairs except for Jane. Mom prayed for this so we would all have a playmate close in age. At times it did seem she had God's ear, because things usually worked out the way she hoped. It probably didn't hurt that on occasion she would say a novena. When there were only nine of us, we were known as Tom and Mike, Mary and Ellen, Billy and Marky, then the "three little kids": Janie, Steve, and Tim.

My oldest brother, Tom, was named after Grandpa George Thomas. His name is officially Thomas George Mueller. Mike was named after Dad's Uncle Mike and Grandpa Peter Mueller. Mary was my Grandma Mueller's name. Ellen Louise was named after Grandma Louise Thomas. I got the name William because, Mom said, "We liked the name Bill." My middle name is Edwin, after Dad. Dad was named after his Grandfather Edwin MacFarland, a drunk, who ran off with a neighbor woman and is buried in a Civil War Veterans Cemetery in Johnson City, Tennessee. Dad said he once asked his mother, "Why did you name me after him?" I don't think she ever gave him a good answer.

As I said, Mark and I were five or six when Mark decided he didn't like being called Marky. So, we agreed at that time to call each other Mark and Bill. I guess it stuck. Ever since, our names have been one syllable. I don't know when the "ie" came off Janie. When Donna and Beth came along that was the end of the "three little kids." About that same time Mark and I decided we weren't going to cry anymore. We started by seeing if we could go all day without tears, then it went to the next and the next day, until there was no more crying. I shared this story with my granddaughter when she was about that age, but I don't think she really appreciated the point of my "no more crying" lesson.

In 1948 before my Grandma Mary Mueller sold Dad the farm, she made Mom and Dad promise that the girls in our family would not be required to do barn chores. My sisters never milked a cow, fed the livestock, pitched manure, or butchered. Even so, though we boys often worked very hard, my sisters had many more rules and much more housework required of them than we boys did. I never did a household chore or babysat until I left home.

In the house, Mary, Ellen, and Jane helped raise the younger siblings in the family, cleaned, and cooked. The girls did much of the harvesting and selling of the produce from our eight-acre garden. They also would help unload wagons when we baled hay or straw.

Donna and Beth, much younger, didn't have to help raise younger kids or move hay. They had many more responsibilities for the garden, our roadside stand, and by then, trips to market to sell our fruit and vegetables.

We boys had altercations all the time. Recently Jane shared the story of one of the few fights she ever had with Mary and Ellen. They were four and three years older than Jane. Dad used to sell semi loads of hay and straw. One time my older sisters in high school thought the guy loading the truck was pretty cute.

They made the mistake of sharing that with Jane. Being her typical telltale middle-school self, she went and told the young man. Mary and Ellen were so angry they sprayed Jane's pillow and sheets with perfume, knowing she hated scents. Jane retaliated by spraying their bedding with fly spray. I don't know how the feud ended.

According to Jane, growing up we boys had a lot more freedom than the girls ever did. That is true; Mark and I never really had a curfew. When we went out Mom would just say to be careful. Looking back, I feel bad that as a teen I wasn't more appreciative or helpful in the house.

Tim shared this story recently. When he and Steve were little, we had an old chest freezer in the old kitchen, no longer being used. Mark lay in the freezer and pretended to be dead. Jane, the prankster, convinced her little brothers that Mark had died and the three of them were responsible to give him a proper funeral. When Tim shared the tale, he explained that it was one of the most traumatic experiences of his life. He was beyond relieved when he learned Mark was still alive.

The American Dream: Land

Grandfather Peter Mueller

Our family's farm was homesteaded in 1842 by Leon Feltz. After thirty years he sold it to Ebenezer Burrows. Peter Mueller came to the United States from Ormont, near Prüm, Germany, in 1890 at age twenty-one. He was supposed to serve a one-year conscription in the German army, but after his going-away party, he secretly boarded a ship and immigrated to America. He was the second of four brothers who immigrated. Eventually, they brought over their parents and sister. Peter worked in a factory for a while in Chicago, but his dream was to farm.

Peter and his younger brother Mike moved to the farm and eventually bought it from Ebenezer Burrows about 1900. In 1906, Peter married my grandmother, Mary McFarland Abresch.

According to Dad, Grandpa Peter Mueller loved America because he was able to own his own farm and train draft horses. In Germany, where he emigrated from, all the farmers used oxen. When we were kids, Dad once found an oxshoe in the field. Grandpa never worked with oxen, so the shoe was from the 1800s.

Grandpa Peter had six adult Percheron draft horses until late in his farming career. Dad said Grandpa also had some Belgians, which were huskier. Each July, Grandpa would call a neighbor to bring over a sire to breed his mares. Gestation was eleven months. The new colts would be born the next June. For the first couple of days after the foal was born, it would follow its mother while she worked the fields. Then, when the mother had a break, the young colt would nurse.

The stallion colts were castrated into geldings. Both mares and geldings learned to pull the various farm implements. Each year, Grandpa Peter raised three or four colts. The young were harnessed with two or three adult horses. Grandpa would sell one or two pairs once they were two years old and trained. A pair of horses was referred to as a team.

When Grandpa Peter had an interested buyer, he let him take the horses home to try them out. Neither Grandpa nor his horses ever worked on The Lord's Day, and he never ate until his horses were first attended to. One Sunday, Grandpa went to go check out his team over the noon hour. The farmer was eating lunch and had left the horses standing in their harnesses. Ticked off, Grandpa brought his horses back home, refusing to sell them to anyone too stupid to properly care for them. Grandpa also would work an expecting mare only a few hours a day. He sold his last team in 1937 and bought his first tractor, an 816 International.

After Grandpa Peter started his family, his brother, Mike, moved to the farm just to the south of ours. That farmhouse later belonged to the Jensens, and then for the last forty-five years to the Fowlers. Mike married a Ruetz girl from a family of businesspeople. Mike, an entrepreneur himself, bought an implement dealership and became very successful. Sadly, at age forty-nine, he died of ether poisoning during hernia surgery.

My Dad lost his cousin and best friend, Hub, after Hub went to live with the Ruetz family in Racine after his father, Mike's, death.

Hub later went on to college and died a pilot during World War II. His older brother Louis became a Catholic Monsignor and served much of his life as a parish priest in South Dakota, where he oversaw the building of two or three Catholic churches. Hub's older sister, Hedwig, became Sister Virginis, who lived to her mid-nineties and was one of the most loving, kind persons I have ever known.

Grandpa Peter was almost fifty when Dad was born. Dad was the seventh son, the second youngest of nine kids. "My father was more like a grandfather," Dad said. "He was never in very good health." Maybe he was just old and worn down. Maybe back then sixty was today's eighty.

Grandpa, according to Dad, wasn't a great farmer, "probably because he gave everything away." He was a deeply devout man, a charter member who helped build St. Sebastian Church in Sturtevant. A neighbor at Grandpa's funeral told Dad, "Peter was the most honest man I have ever known." Shortly before Dad died, he was asked, "What do you want to be remembered for?" His response was, "I want to be remembered for being honest."

The lessons my Grandfather Peter and then Dad taught their children were surely different from the way some people were raised. Dad used to tell about one neighbor boy who would cheat at every opportunity. One time some kids were playing in the creek. This boy hid one of the swimmer's bikes, then later claimed it for himself. Dad bought it from him at a bargain price, not knowing its origin. Asparagus used to grow in the roadside ditches. The plants came from droppings of birds roosting on the rural fence lines. One day, this same neighbor kid saw some people picking asparagus and told them that the ditches had just been sprayed and the asparagus they had already picked wasn't safe to eat. As soon as they left, he took the discarded asparagus home to his family.

During the depression, Grandpa Peter, like everyone else, was just trying to survive. In his last few years, he took a job in town. This is how Grandma Mary received Social Security until she died.

Several of Dad's older brothers were single and still working on the farm. Anyone living at home who had a job was required to pay rent. Dad didn't think that was right. In addition to working off the farm, he spent a lot of time still laboring at home.

Dad believed his father never encouraged any of his kids to get ahead. "For sure, he never put a high value on education," Dad said. Grandma Mary knew her son Edwin was smart and thought he should attend high school. Grandpa Peter relented, but Dad would have to find his way to and from school. St. Catherine High School was eight miles from home. Grandpa Peter and four or five neighbors used to take turns delivering their milk to Racine, so Dad rode with them to school. One day each week, Dad was late for school because one of the farmers was still using a wagon and horses to make the delivery for his turn. Most days, to get home, he rode with a family friend who worked in a factory in Racine.

With six older brothers, some still living at home, Dad grew up feeling that he had several fathers always telling him what to do. Dad graduated at age seventeen and decided to see the world, so he and a friend hopped on a train heading west. The friend was desperate to leave his abusive, drunken father. They left without telling anyone and were gone four months. When Dad returned home, he didn't know what kind of reception he was going to get with his scruffy beard and tattered clothes. Dad's best friend, Champ, not recognizing him, growled as he approached. When Dad called him by name, the dog went nuts with joy. Next Dad met his father in the dooryard. Peter was not usually an emotional person. For the first time ever, Peter gave Dad a hug and told him he loved him.

Peter died of what they called back then hardening of the arteries.

Grandmother Mary Mueller

Mary Maud McFarland was born in Kenosha County, Wisconsin, on February 2, 1876, the one-hundredth birthday year of the United States. She grew up in Fort Atkinson and Plainfield. At eighteen, she married Bill

Abresch, her senior by about twenty years, and they had two sons, John and Sam. Bill died of tuberculosis, leaving Mary a widow at age twenty. After Bill's death, Mary lived in a shack down near Pete Ingrouille, whose wife was Bill's sister. Their son, Cliff, a few years older than Dad, used to visit Grandma when we were kids. I always thought it was interesting that he called her Aunt Mary. She was Cliff's aunt by marriage.

To survive, Mary did cleaning and laundry for some of the neighbors. My Grandfather Peter used to see her walk by with her two little boys, John and Sam, in tow. One day, he asked Mary if she would be willing to be a housekeeper for Mike and him. So, for four dollars a week plus room and board, she moved into the Mueller mansion. Grandma used to always joke, "They got behind on my pay, so they decided one of them should marry me." She married Peter, my grandfather, and had seven more children. They were Ethel, Francis (France), Al, Fred (Freddy), Henry (Hank), Edwin (Red, my Dad), and Josephine (Josie).

Al, eight years older, was Dad's hero. He was smart, adventurous, had a great sense of humor, and really took an interest in his little brother Red. Grandma also raised her son Sam's two children, Ann and Bill Abresch. To Dad, they were like a little brother and sister.

Dad, Edwin (nicknamed Red), the youngest boy, eventually bought the farm from Grandma Mary in 1948, and she continued to live in the house with them.

By 1956, Mom and Dad had seven kids, and that's when Grandma Mary decided to move out. Dad wanted to build her a small home to the northwest of the house. His thinking was that after she died, it would be something they could continue to use. She wouldn't hear of it; she preferred he just buy her a trailer to live out her days, which turned out to be almost twenty years.

Grandma Mary had an oil-burning furnace in her trailer. It was just inside the front door to the left. Grandma was kept warm okay, but it sure didn't help keep the water pipes from freezing when it was below zero. Dad, on occasion, used to have to thaw pipes on the coldest night of the year. At Halloween we would get some soot from Grandma's oil burner when we needed a beard for our costume.

Dad strung a wire running from Grandma's trailer connecting intercoms in both the house and trailer. This was so if there was ever an emergency, or Grandma needed anything, she could just call. I don't know if it ever served its purpose, but we kids sure enjoyed playing with it.

My Uncle Sam Abresch, Grandma's second son, a divorcé, lived with her in the trailer for most of those years. He used to go to Panama in the winter to visit his son, Bill, who was a postmaster for the U.S. Government. I remember Sam brought back straw hats for us kids and one time a conch shell for Grandma.

Once, my brother Mike was preparing Uncle Sam's flower garden for planting when he knocked Grandma Mary's trailer off its concrete pad. To make a smooth turn while disking a field, the driver locks up either the right or left brake on the tractor while spinning the steering wheel, giving him a nice clean turn. As Mike approached the trailer, the tractor's big back wheel slid on a pie tin, causing the crash into Grandma's home. Everyone inside came out, thinking there had been an earthquake.

Grandma's trailer was always somewhere we went to get out of the house. On Sunday nights, if we kids didn't want to watch *Bonanza* at home, we could go out to the trailer and watch *The Ed Sullivan Show* with Grandma, who loved music. If we wanted to see the Beatles or Elvis, we had to watch Ed Sullivan with her. If we didn't like the television show at our house, we watched television with Grandma until *The Lawrence Welk Show* came on. Grandma loved it, but we didn't.

Some of the earliest shows I remember were *Combat*, a World War II series, followed by *McHale's Navy* starring Ernest Borgnine and Tim Conway. The *Andy Griffith Show* and *Dick Van Dyke Show* were favorites. Sundays at 6:30 p.m. was *The Wonderful World of Disney* on NBC. Grandma usually had plenty of us kids to keep her company on those weekend nights, and she always had store-bought sugar cookies for us to eat. That probably contributed to the sweet tooth I happily nourish today.

Grandma lived to be 98. She died August 15, 1974. If she had lived another year-and-a-half she would have died in America's bicentennial year. She was in pretty good health, and we all thought she was going to make it to one hundred. Back then, people rarely lived to be that old. She suffered a stroke on August 12, 1974, and died in the hospital three days later. Grandma was always afraid she was going to die in February. Each year, when she got through that month, she believed she had another year. She had a superstitious nature, believing that bad events such as accidents, illnesses, or death came in threes. She would always relax after the third person died, because it wasn't her turn yet.

Grandma used to peel apples for Mom's pies, sew on buttons, and patch our clothes when needed. Her woven rugs were made by a lady in Racine, but Grandma made her own braided rag rugs. Grandma started these by ripping old clothes into strips, sewing the ends together, and rolling them into what they called rag balls. Then with a hollow metal tool she braided these strips into beautiful, durable rugs. When I was five years old, Mom sent Grandma my favorite shirt for her to sew on a new button. She thought the shirt was scrap to be used for one of her rugs. When I saw that my prized possession was now part of Grandma's rag ball collection, I was devastated and shed a few tears that I had promised Mark I wouldn't shed anymore.

Grandma Mary used to love to go for rides. Mom always said, "Anytime a car left our yard, Grandma was a passenger."

Grandma memorized countless poems and stories to recite. Locally she was well known for what she called her "readings" or "recitations." People from all around attended Pike River School functions to listen.

When I was little, Grandma would both whistle and sing to me the first verse of *Billy Boy*. I know as a little boy from a big family it sure made me feel special. Here is the song:

Oh, where have you been, Billy Boy, Billy Boy?
Oh, where have you been, Charming Billy?
I have been to seek a wife, She's the joy of my life,
She's a young thing, And cannot leave her mother.

As a small boy, I also remember once or twice Grandma took me to celebrate my birthday at the Country Kitchen restaurant, which was on the south end of our farm. It was owned by our neighbor Annetta Ramcke, a wonderful, loving woman.

Grandfather George Thomas

George Thomas was Mom's father. Even though Thomas can be a Welsh name, George's grandfather and grandmother Peter and Mary emigrated from Uderdorf, Germany. So the name Thomas is also German. Their son Nicholas, my great-grandfather, was a second-generation German farmer who believed sports were foolishness.

Nicholas's son, my Grandfather George, as a young man from Somers Township, was a sensational baseball player. When Nicholas died, his family found in his belongings a letter from the Chicago Cubs asking George to come to try out for their team. For Grandpa Thomas, it's a shame this dream was never realized. For us, we should all be thankful Great-Grandpa Nicholas was so heartless, or we might not be here today.

Grandpa married Magdelena Feest in October 1908. They were blessed with Mildred, Vincent (Binny), Marie, and Charlie, before she died in 1915. George needed help raising his four children. According to Mom, after two or three dates he married my grandmother, Louise Robers of Burlington in April of 1920. Together they had eleven more children.

9

George Jr. died at a year old, about the time Marcella, my mother, was born in 1922. Next were Alice, Joe, Jerry, Jean, Ralph, Leo, Rita, Kathy, and Annie.

Grandpa Thomas was the town clerk of Somers for thirty years. He had a sanguine personality; he loved people and taught his kids to enjoy life. "If he was dressed up, the children couldn't go," Mom always said. "If he wasn't, he took his kids everywhere."

Mom grew up in an era when many families, especially Germans, had archaic ideas and thought only their boys should be taught to play cards and pursue enjoyment in living. Grandpa George didn't agree, and he shared his love of life with both his girls and his boys. Under George's tutelage, Mom became an excellent Sheepshead player. Mom in turn taught all of us kids how to play, some more successfully than others.

Grandpa George died of colon cancer on September 25, 1942, during World War II, four years before Mom and Dad were married. Mom was very close to her Dad and would sometimes reminisce about the lessons he taught and his love for children. I would love to have known him.

Grandmother Louise Thomas

Grandma Louise's grandparents came from Westphalia, a region of Germany. Louise, my grandmother, was born June 1, 1894. She grew up in Burlington and died July 11, 1969, of a heart attack. At the time, I was sixteen. Even though I saw Grandma Louise often when I was growing up, I never knew her very well. Mom explained that Grandma raised fourteen children, plus her granddaughter. By the time most of her sixty-plus grandkids came along, she didn't want to spend much time with kids. Whenever we were at her house, she would shoo the kids outside or to a different room in the house so the adults could visit.

Grandma Louise owned thirty-five acres on Wood Road, a couple of miles from our farm. During the 1960s, the State of Wisconsin decided it needed a university in the Kenosha and Racine area to serve the residents of southeast Wisconsin. Using Eminent Domain, officials forced Grandma and many of her neighbors to sell their farms and homes and relocate. Grandma bought a home in Kenosha and lived there until her death.

Mom's oldest brother, Uncle Binney, a bachelor, stayed on the farm after Grandma moved. Someone came in one day and stole his bathtub, which necessitated his move sooner than he had planned. The University of Wisconsin-Parkside was built soon after. Grandma's farm was located by the current heating plant on the northeast corner of the University.

Old Grandpa Lichter, our friend Ray Lichter's father, lived in a little house on the west edge of the new campus. Because of his age, they told him he could stay put until he died. I think he reach his nineties, longer than they expected, so they kicked him out, too.

After Grandma Louise died, Mom, who was a lot like her father, sanguine and fun-loving, became her family's matriarch, coordinating celebrations and card-playing marathons until she died January 11, 2017.

Cousins

Mom claimed she was from a family of fourteen kids because that many lived to adulthood. Dad was from a family of nine children. Most of their siblings were married, so growing up I had forty aunts and uncles and I had eighty first cousins. There was a forty-year range from my oldest to youngest first cousins.

Some of our cousins were close in age and were our good friends. Rich and Alan Karls, Ray Mueller, Pat and John Yacukowicz, and Mary Lynn Penza were all close to Tom and Mike. Frank Penza, Mark, and I spent a lot of time together growing up.

My cousin Frank Penza was in a band the summer before we started eighth grade. He played at his sister Joan's wedding. They had live music at the reception, then they set up a small room for the younger kids and Frank's group performed. My sister Jane thought *Do Wah Diddy* was the only song they knew. She said, "They had the chorus down, but didn't know all the verses," Jane said. "I was sure the only song they could play was *Hanky Panky*." As middle schoolers we were having fun and didn't really care.

It reminds me of the *Happy Days* episode where Richie Cunningham and his friends started their own band. They sounded pretty good, so they were hired to play at a fraternity party. It went well until they started playing the one song they knew repeatedly.

At the time Frank's band didn't have a name. I remember my brothers and sisters and I tried to come up with one. Here are a couple my sisters came up with: *Frank and Beans*, and *Frank the Crank and The Turn Overs*. Maybe you had be a farm kid to fully appreciate the second one. Before electric ignitions and keys were invented, hand cranks were used to start cars, trucks, and tractors. To start it you had to do what was called "turn it over."

Meet the Neighbors

The majority of our neighbors were wonderful people. These were the Thoms, Hartigs, Prednys, Jensens, Ramckes, Biexes, Corbetts, Rohners, Funks, Ingrouilles, Teuschers, Gagnons, Keens, Klinkhammers, Rasmussens, Gauchels, Mandernicks, and Youngs, just to name a few.

Our most interesting neighbors were a sister and brother a couple of years older than Dad, Merle and Mert Fink. They were fraternal twins who saw life in shades of gray.

When kids had necking sessions parked by Lake Michigan, we called that "watching the submarine races." Late one night, a local deputy spotted a car in Fink's field. Assuming it was local teenagers parking, he planned to send them on their way. But that was until he interrupted Merle's session. She accused him of harassing innocent folks and trespassing on private property.

Merle never married, and she always worked a job in town. She cohabitated decades before it became common practice. When her first live-in died, she inherited his money. After this happened one or two more times, Merle died a rich woman.

Mert married "Saint" Elsie, a sweet person who raised two nice boys in spite of her husband. Merle and Mert lived a mile from each other and didn't get along, although they did reconcile in their old age. This was fortunate for Mert's kids, because when their Aunt Merle died, they and their first cousin inherited a considerable sum.

Mom was always anxious to get us out from underfoot, unless it was to go see Mert. Mark and I used to visit Mert so we could hear Mert swear. His language was quite colorful. Mom was always disappointed whenever Dad made a shrewd deal with Mert, because it never worked out for us.

One time, Mert lent his boar to Dad to breed a couple of sows. Mert didn't need it, so Dad fed and cared for it all winter until it was needed to service Mert's sows in the spring. Another time Dad needed a bull to breed his heifers, his young cows. By the time Mert finally picked up the bull, it had gained several hundred pounds from Dad's care. Whenever Mert borrowed our equipment, we usually had to retrieve it and fix whatever got broken. I remember one time getting our hay wagon out from a three-feet-deep manure yard.

Mert wasn't really meant to be a dairy farmer. Routine is a high priority for anyone who milks cows, or else milk production suffers. Most farmers milk at dawn and again in late afternoon. To prevent injuring a cow's teats, the milking machine is only used for three or four minutes on each cow twice a day. Mert didn't have a set schedule for milking and didn't pay too close attention to how long a milking machine hung on a cow. He used to add water to the milk tank then say, "It all weighs." His ground feed was a light green color, because he added hay to his corn and oat mixture, as opposed to having pure grains.

When Mark and I were in middle school, we worked for Mert milking his grade B herd of cows. Grade B meant the milk was used for making cheese rather than for drinking. Mert died thirty-five years ago, and still owes me twenty dollars in back pay.

Once Mark and our friend, Mike Chiappe, stopped down to Mert's place. They were probably fourteen or fifteen at the time. Mert had just bought an Angus bull. These are black and produce a smaller calf. Farmers often breed their first-calf heifers to an Angus to make the birthing easier for both mother and calf. Mert had high gates on his old red pickup truck with the angry bull in the back. Its explosive bucking and jumping had Mike, a city kid, believing the truck was going to tip over.

Dairy bulls can be deadly, so farmers often put a steel ring that weighs one-third of a pound in the animal's nose to better control it. For the same reason, Mert's plan was to put a ring in the nose of his Angus bull. You can imagine how five or six ounces of metal stuck in your nose would affect your attitude.

Harvey was Mert's hired man. He was a nice old guy, small, short on education, but fearless. When they finally got the bull in the barn, it knocked poor Harvey into the manger. I guess when you are trying to direct an irate fifteen-hundred-pound beast you need a better weapon than a pitchfork.

Eventually the bull was locked in a stanchion, a device made for milk cows. Two bars hold the cow's neck in place while being milked. Stanchions are not made for bulls, especially those in a fury. This bull had never been in a stanchion before, and was going crazy, throwing its body left and right.

Mert dropped the tiny screw that was necessary to lock the ring in the bull's nose. When he ran to his workroom to find another, he told my brother Mark and our friend Mike Chiappe to hold the rope tight around the animal's neck.

In Mert's absence, the bull jumped one last time, coughed and crumpled to the floor. When Mert came rushing back he yelled, "Get the rope off him, you choked him to death!" What really happened was the bull died of a broken neck from throwing himself back and forth in the stanchion. This wasn't what Mert had planned for the bull.

I saw Mike Chiappe at our forty-fifth high school class reunion. He said, "That was the single most traumatic experience of my life."

Bull meat is rank. I was always told the only thing bull meat could be used for was to make bologna, to disguise the taste. Mert did find someone to butcher and save the meat.

Once when Mert was shipping a steer for Dad, he used a wooden ladder for a gate. This closed off part of our barn floor, which should have made loading the steer onto the truck an easier task. With his cattle prod, Mert gleefully ran the frightened steer right through the ladder. After that, loading the terror-stricken animal onto the truck was quite a chore. Not surprisingly, when Dad got home from work, he was not too pleased with his broken ladder or his neighbor.

When it was time to ship animals to market, Dad would either call a trucker or have a neighbor take his animals along with theirs. Once he shipped a nice healthy calf along with someone's sickly one. When the check arrived, it was much smaller than it should have been. Dad was sure the hauler switched calves and gave him the money for the sickly one.

Dad shared the story of when Mert built his new house. When digging the new well, they hit water at only twenty or thirty feet. Normally a well is one hundred or more feet deep, so you get clean, drinkable water. Mert didn't want to spend any more money, so he told the well digger the well was deep enough. The driller said, "It has to go deeper," but Mert insisted. The well driller said, "Let's pump it all night and see how it looks in the morning."

When they returned the next day to check, Mert's farm pond across the road was empty.

The Teuscher Sisters

Ruth and Margaret Teuscher were unmarried sisters. Ruth, an English teacher, and Margaret, a home economics teacher, both taught in the Racine public schools. Ruth was a nationally known textbook author. Margaret, in retirement, was the president of the Wisconsin Retired Teachers Association. In 1935 they purchased forty acres a mile-and-a-half south of our farm along Highway 31, just west of Petrifying Springs Park. The sisters named their purchase Hawthorn Hollow, after the hawthorn trees that they liked on the property.

Ruth and Margaret, both historians and naturalists, developed their land so they could share their passions with the public. In 1956 the sisters built a Williamsburg colonial-style house on the property.

14

In 1967, the sisters donated their land and buildings to the Hyslop Foundation to be a nature sanctuary and arboretum. A short time later, the Foundation moved three of Somers Township's most historic buildings onto the premises. These were the 1859 Somers Town Hall, the 1847 Pike River School, and the second 1906 Pike River School. The schools had been built right next to Pike River and named after it. Pike River is the creek that also runs through our farm upstream from where the schools were built. Pike River eventually drains into Lake Michigan.

Ruth's contributions to Somers Township were significant. During the 1960s and 1970s, she recorded much of Somers' history dating back to the 1800s. Ruth knew that contemporary primary sources, which are people's first-hand accounts, are generally most reliable when we look at our past. This is why Ruth was thrilled when she met Mary (MacFarland) Mueller (1876-1974), my Dad's mom.

Grandma Mary Mueller was well known locally for her readings. At community gatherings she entertained her neighbors and friends with poems and short stories she recited from memory.

Much of Ruth's Somers Township history came from Grandma Mary, who lived in Somers Township most of her life, and whose recall was sharp to the very end of her ninety-eight years. Over time, Ruth and Grandma became good friends and in the late 1960s Grandma donated her eight-foot 1846 canvas map of the Wisconsin Territory to Ruth Teuscher and the Hyslop Foundation.

When I was a junior in the 1970-1971 school year, I wrote a paper for one of my classes. The subject was, "Hawthorn Hollow and Ruth Teuscher." Ruth and I became friends, and sometimes I would stop for a visit with Ruth and a hike on the property. On more than one occasion Ruth lent me the keys to the Town Hall and both school buildings so I could give myself a personal tour of the grounds.

I went to see Ruth in late 1981 or early 1982. I knew of her sister's death the previous year. During our visit, Ruth shared with me that her horse, Major, had died. They had been companions for thirty-five years. Ruth explained how difficult that year had been and how she missed her loyal Major. She never mentioned the loss of her sister, Margaret, that same year, although they had been lifelong roommates.

Ruth, born in 1894, died in 1988 at the age of ninety-four. Margaret, born in 1896, preceded her sister in death in 1981 at age eighty-four.

Norm Miller

Norm Miller was Dad's best friend and my second cousin. Norm's Grandfather Frank and my Grandpa Peter were brothers. Norm started his career as a truck farmer raising potatoes and cabbage. Because of Norm's bad back, his doctor insisted he find another line of work.

In 1956 Norm bought a potato planter from a man in Milwaukee who was leaving farming to start a driving range and miniature golf course. When this person saw Norm's great location on the edge of Racine, with its wide-open flat land, he encouraged Norm to start a driving range, too. In the spring of 1957, with a hand seeder, Norm and his brother Frank planted ten acres of grass instead of potatoes. This became the driving range. In 1958, the next summer, he opened his miniature golf course. This new business became known as the Durand Driving Range and Miniature Golf. It was scenic, roomy, well kept, fun, and challenging. Norm's, as we called it, provided great entertainment and recreation for us Mueller kids growing up. When we weren't playing softball, we spent many summer evenings with Norm and his son, Bob.

We would pay for our first game, then they never charged us for a second game or a bucket of balls. Mark, Jane, and I were pretty competitive: first, fighting over which ball we got: blue, green, red, or orange; then, who had the best score or which hole-in-one was the toughest to get. I'm sure Norm and Bob enjoyed watching our antics. Miniature golf was also a great date night. The fees were reasonable, and we could show off our athleticism. This was easy when our dates had never seen a putter before. The big crowds all season long made Durand Driving Range and Miniature Golf a local success that lasted forty years. In 1996 Norm sold his one-hundred-twenty acres. A Menard's store now sits on what was once Norm's farm.

I rarely golf today. When I do, putting is the only decent part of my game, thanks to you, Norm. He was always so nice and interested in each member of our family. For many years Norm, his wife, Phyllis, and Mom and Dad used to go out to eat at least once a month. In later years, with Bob's assistance, they were still able to enjoy these outings.

The Bennetts

We got a call one day that our pigs were in the upscale neighborhood on Corbett Road rooting up people's lawns. These pigs didn't belong to us, but Dad went over and brought the pair home anyway. Because there wasn't much livestock in our neighborhood, it didn't take long to figure that these animals belonged to the Bennetts, the hillbillies who lived a half mile east of where the destruction had happened.

When Bennett, his son, and a friend came to retrieve their hogs, they were so drunk they could barely stand. Dad later said, "Between the three of them they didn't have the brains combined of the two pigs they came to get." After some discussion the three decided they were going to shoot and butcher the pigs on the spot. Dad said, "You can't eat boar meat; it is rank and unfit for human consumption." One of the guys responded, "No problem, we will castrate it and the meat will taste just fine."

One of them pulled out a loaded revolver. With concrete everywhere, this inebriated guy didn't understand the concept of ricochets. From the front he tried aiming at the pig's head. It was moving too much, so one of the others got behind the hog, looking up the barrel of the gun, and tried to get it to stand still so the first could shoot it. Dad and my little sister Donna quickly left the barn, hoping one of the men inside didn't get shot.

Rita, Joanne, and Bernie

Recently Rita Mason, a neighbor, shared this story with me. Sixty years ago, Rita found me at age three out for a walk on Highway 31. She brought me up to our house and when Mom answered the door, inquired if this was where I lived. Mom asked where Rita found me. "Out on the road." Mom's response was, "The older kids were supposed to be watching him." Later we went to school with the Mason kids. Rita and Mom became good friends.

Joanne Thom Ramcke shared the story about moving from the trailer park and her forty playmates in town to the lonely house in the country across the highway from Dad's farm. At the time, she was eleven, an only child. I was checking out the new neighbors. Being three and a curious kid, I crossed the highway again and after I climbed up onto the front step, Joanne discovered me looking through the window of their front door. I was watching the black-and-white television set — we didn't have one yet. Joanne was sure God had sent her a new little brother. She was sadly disappointed when her Mom and Dad wouldn't let her keep me and returned me back home across the road. Guess I had a wandering spirit.

Bernie Klinkhammer had the rural Racine Journal paper route for many years. In the summer when he took his vacation, we more than once subbed for him. That was a hoot: he had more than 100 subscribing patrons.

Dad's herd,
1955 or 1956.

Donna and Beth with Sniffer.

Audrey with our Guernsey cow.

The Mueller chickens, about the 1970s.

Chapter 2: Farm Life

Mark, a year younger than I was, was the first of us boys who wanted to milk the cow, so at age nine and ten, Mark and I started. We didn't have much hand strength, so milking two gallons took a half hour to complete. When we took too long, Rosie would get nervous and swat us in the face. Her tail wasn't always dry or clean. The swatting was a warning that if we didn't hurry up, she was going to kick over the milk, or worse yet, put her foot in the pail. Mom would get pretty upset anytime we came from the barn with no milk. Steve and Tim later took over the job reluctantly when Mark and I became busy with sports and off-the-farm jobs.

As I've said, Dad bought Grandma Mueller's farm in 1948. It was ninety acres. He later bought six acres more across Highway 31 to the east of our front yard. This made the total ninety-six acres. Pike River ran through near the western edge of the farm with five acres or so on the other side. Seventy-five yards from the farm's northern boundary stood our seven-acre woods. It runs east to west parallel to Highway KR. Forty yards west of the trees stood a giant oak all by itself in the field.

Our cow's pasture and lane were along the southern border of the farm, which might have been eight acres total. About halfway down to the creek just a few yards north stood another huge tree, I'm guessing also an oak. We had sixty-five to seventy acres that were tillable.

The Wilks brothers, Al and Norm, started renting Dad's land to farm in 1968. Norm is now gone, but their operation is still headed by Al. Today they run six thousand acres.

Livestock — and a Parakeet

Grandpa Peter Mueller had twelve cows, all milked by hand. Dad milked twenty cows from 1953 to 1956. He added more concrete to the south end of the cow barn and added eight more stanchions. Then he added an automated milking system. In the 1950s and 1960s, twenty to thirty cows per herd was pretty typical.

Like most dairy farmers, he milked Holstein cows. Though they eat more feed, they produce larger quantities of milk. Back then, cows were milked two times each day, early morning and early evening.

My wife, Audrey, grew up on a dairy farm near Janesville. In the 1960s and 1970s they milked eighty cows; that was considered a big operation at that time. Today a farm just five miles east of her homestead has a herd with five-thousand Holstein cows.

Every milk cow gives birth to a new calf every year, traditionally in early summer. Some farmers own their own bull or bulls for breeding their cows. Many farmers choose to artificially inseminate their cattle, if they have a small number of cows or don't want to mess with a dairy bull that can be mean and dangerous.

Farmers stop milking a cow, called drying them up, six to eight weeks before the delivery of her next calf. This prepares the mother to have a healthy calf, and it also allows her to produce a lot of milk when she freshens or births her calf.

Dad had a heifer named Buttons that was bred too young. Somehow a bull got to her before she was old enough and she became pregnant. Because she was not big enough, she had a difficult delivery. The veterinarian advised that Buttons not be bred a second time, because she was going to be unable to have any more calves.

After Buttons was milked for a year, instead of breeding her, she was fattened to be butchered. She was only three years old and her meat would be prime. So, when she was big enough, Dad decided it was time. They cut a tree from the woods and trimmed all the limbs making it into a log to lay across the upper beams above the barn floor. From here he planned to do the butchering. Because this was Buttons, our family pet, Dad left strict instructions that none of the little kids should be permitted to come to the barn while he and his friend Jim were working. At five years old, I was somehow able to reach the barn. Surprised at what I saw, I asked Dad what he was doing. His answer worked for this small boy: "I am taking off Button's overcoat," Dad replied.

Once, our Guernsey milk cow got out of our pasture and found her way down to Mert's across the road, where she was impregnated by his Holstein bull. Nine months later she had a heifer calf. Most dairy farmers milked Holsteins, some preferred Guernseys. None were interested in a mixed breed. Dad knew she would not bring a good price if he shipped her to market. Joe, a friend from work, assured Dad, "We can butcher this cow ourselves." This time I was a teenager, able to help. When we got her hanging from the log, Joe asked Dad, "What do we do next?"

I know of four people who worked for Dad. One was Al Pardington, who was called Cowboy because he wore cowboy boots. Years later we went to visit him; he went on to become a successful realtor in Rhinelander. Another was Bob Gagnon, son of Dad's good friend Buster. Dad called him Flying Bob because he drove the tractor so fast. Buster worked for J.I. Case Company. He was a magician with machinery and helped Dad with his tractors whenever needed. When Buster died, my brother Mark got his cider press, which our family still uses today when we make apple cider.

Two other hired men who lived with us were John, the one my older siblings were afraid of, and Big John, a kindly giant who had a glass eye. On occasion he would remove it and show it to Tom and Mike. They said he ate a whole box of cereal in a big mixing bowl for breakfast. Sometimes when working with a cow it is necessary to lean into them, to make room to wash their teats or to put on the milking machine. According to Dad, Big John once accidentally knocked a cow over and broke her leg.

One of Dad's hired men wasn't washing the milking equipment properly, so the bacteria count grew too high. The milk inspector was going to downgrade Dad's milk classification from Grade A to Grade B. With all the extra work and the headaches associated with milking cows, Dad decided it wasn't worth it. In 1956, when I was three years old, Dad sold his herd. Big John was crushed when his services were no longer needed.

When Dad shipped his cows, he asked the trucker to look for a Guernsey that we could buy for our family's source of milk. At the Milwaukee stockyard, the hauler found a heifer that was to be butchered. Dad bought her and she became Pinky, our faithful milk provider for twelve years. She was followed by her daughter Rosie whom we also had for many years. They provided milk for our family and Mom's milk customers for more than twenty years.

Two neighbors, Annetta Ramcke and Freda Malowitz, were Mom's best longtime customers and good friends. Annetta owned the Country Kitchen restaurant next to our farm; she used our fresh milk and cream in many of her homemade dishes and pastries. Freda was driving past our farm one day and saw our cattle. She stopped and inquired about buying milk from Mom. Freda and her husband, Gus, who were born and raised in Lithuania, didn't need the milk as fresh because they used the cream-laden milk to make cheese. Years later, Freda was disappointed when Dad, at age sixty-two, decided to quit milking.

Dad preferred having a Guernsey for the family cow. She was not as big as a black-and-white Holstein, but gentler and produced a high butterfat or cream count. We always had our cow, Rosie, bred to freshen, or have a calf, in late spring or early summer. A cow produces a lot of milk after having a calf, when she gets fresh green pasture, good ground feed, and gentle treatment. Each summer our cow would give up to five gallons of milk each day.

Usually we boys did the milking in the evening. Dad milked and did the other barn chores before he went to work in the morning. Dad could milk a couple of gallons in what seemed like two or three minutes. We milked sitting on a little three-legged stool, always on the right side of the cow.

First, we gave her some ground feed. We used a mix of barley and oats, or corn and oats. Before milking, we washed off her teats. We boys did all the milking morning and night in the summertime when our cow was giving the most milk.

In the fall when we went back to school, Dad started milking in the mornings again. Rosie never was happy to see him return. Because he was so strong, his hands hurt the cow's teats and she wouldn't stand still very well until she once again got used to him bruising her udder.

One summer Dad didn't have any calves. The fence was in need of repair, so we put Rosie out in the hay field west of the house. She was chained, and once a day we would move her to a section of fresh alfalfa. We brought her water and ground feed. She was a patient and gentle cow. Twice a day, on the milk stool we would sit next to her. She would stand quietly until we were finished milking. Normally a cow would never stand still in an open field while you milked her.

Every once in a while, Dad would splurge. At an auction he once bought a young Blue Roan cow we named Blue Belle, a milking Shorthorn that he liked. She didn't produce as much milk, with little cream. I am surprised Mom would put up with a real pretty cow that wasn't suitable for her milk customers. Blue Belle did have a cute bull calf named Little Mike because he was born on Mike's birthday. But they didn't stay on the farm too long.

Dad said that raising calves was his favorite part of farming. Dad raised six to eight calves each winter. These were Holstein bull calves that became steers when they were castrated. He also raised some Angus-Holstein crossbreds.

Most of those calves Dad bought from Ray Lichter or his brother Ed Lichter. I remember sometimes he would pay $10 for a two- or three-day-old calf. We used to love to go with Dad on these adventures to pick up calves. Back then, we didn't have a pickup truck, so we would put them in the back of our Rambler station wagon. When Dad bought baby pigs, they would go into a gunnysack and be transported in the back of the same car.

Every spring we walked the entire electric fence line making repairs. Some years we extended our pasture across the creek, making the fence more than a half a mile in length. Before we let the calves out of the barn, we tied strips of rag on the fence, so they would know their boundaries. Letting these 400-pound calves out of the barn for the first time was one of my favorite events on the farm. Watching them eat fresh green grass for the first time in a whole new world was a thrill.

Making a halter from a rope, we would lead them outside, one calf at a time. Some got very excited and would kick, jump, and run until they got tired. Once the initial shock wore off, the calf would start to eat grass or investigate its new environment. We made sure each calf was settled down before we would let them anywhere near the electric fence.

When they did first touch the wire, they touched it with their nose. That first jolt from the hot wire would send them into a frenzy. We held the rope tight, so they wouldn't knock the fence down in their panic. The bigger the calf, the bigger the challenge it was to break them to the pasture. After the calf had been shocked two or three times, it knew the fence was off limits. We then walked them along the fence line, their boundary. It was fun watching the cows and calves in the pasture leisurely grazing after spending all winter cooped up in the barn.

Sometimes we ran electric current from both ends of the pasture, so that the current would be stronger and keep the livestock in when they got a quarter of a mile from the barn. One time we had the wire running above our manure pile from the silo to the southeast side of the barn. I didn't notice the sagging line, when I accidentally touched it with my head. Because I was standing in water, the jolt felt like I got kicked in the head. Soon I realized I was on my hands and knees in six inches of manure soup.

On the west side of the cow barn we kept two pigs. We used them mainly to clean up the slop, leftover food from the house. The slop bucket was kept under the sink. The pigs also ate ground feed. Our pigpen was fifteen by twelve feet. In the northwest corner was a ten-inch high, four by six-foot platform for them to sleep on. In the pigpen, the pigs kept themselves relatively clean. Sometimes we would throw straw on the platform for the pigs to stay warm.

Pig manure has very little straw in it and is heavy. We always used a scoop shovel when cleaning hog pens. A manure fork would have been about as practical as using a dinner fork for eating soup.

Mom's rule was we were never going to have pigs where they could be smelled from the house or yard. Pig manure smells bad. Audrey's family raised hogs, milked eighty cows, and had 6,000 laying hens. She claims chicken manure is the worst. Manure is manure!

Years ago, farmers used to let market hogs grow to almost 300 pounds. Dad had friends, originally from Eastern Europe, who used to buy our pigs when they were ready to butcher, along with a bale of straw. They cut the pig's throat, then would hold it by the ear and catch the blood for blood sausage. Once the pig was dead, the men lit the straw to burn off the pig's hair.

One summer when I was really young, Dad had nine sows, with their litters numbering one hundred. He wanted to get them out of the sun, so he fenced in part of our seven-acre woods. The sows ate all the young trees, so when I was growing up part of our timber had only big established trees and new growth, no mid-sized trees. The summer I was sixteen we had some pigs fenced in a quarter acre on the far southeast section of the woods. They were moved back to the barn when neighbor dogs bothered them. I remember the hog's ears were badly cut up.

Often when farmers have pigs outside, they put three or four hog rings in their snout to keep them from rooting. Otherwise they can tear up a lot of ground. I have often wondered when I see people with multiple rings in their nose if they wear them for the same reason.

My fifth birthday present was Fuzzy, an adorable lamb we all fell in love with. One day she was grazing in our orchard, tied to an apple tree. Nero and Beaver, the German Shepherds belonging to the Jensens next door, came over and killed her. The Jensens were good neighbors, but Dad lost it. He thought the dogs should have been put to sleep. Jensens did pay for poor Fuzzy. Dad told Jerry Jensen that if he ever saw the dogs on our farm again, they would be buried right where they died.

More than a couple of stray dogs died on our farm when they got caught chasing or killing our livestock. Dad once even put down one of his own dogs for the same crime. "Once they taste blood," he said, "they can never ever be trusted again."

When I was little we had a half-acre fenced-in lot north of our house that kept a few sheep. It was woven hog wire thirty inches high with a strand of barbed-wire on top. The sheep would graze during the summer and would escape frequently. Mom draped several old coats in various places around the fence. The sheep thought these were sentries, and they never got out again.

Have you ever heard the saying, "A sick sheep is a dead sheep"? Sheep seem pretty stupid, but a person who raises sheep recently told me that sheep are tougher than other farm animals and hide their illness. I guess in the wild when they get sick they just wait for another animal to come and eat them.

Audrey and I have friends, Allan and Barb, who raised sheep. They had fifty ewes that lambed each year, in late winter. Each December, Allan and Barb sheared their sheep. This prevented the ewes from giving birth to their young out in a snowbank. Because they were cold, they looked for a warm barn to have their young in.

Another time my younger brother Steve got a black lamb for his birthday. Somehow it strayed into the rented horse pen of Black Jack, Mr. Weinkauf's horse. The lamb was kicked by Black Jack and didn't live long, a sad event for Steve and us kids.

One day when I was eleven or twelve, Hank Weinkauf had stopped, inquiring as to whether he could board a horse in our barn. At the time he offered Dad a pretty good boarding fee. I think it was $35 a month for Black Jack to stay.

He was a stallion Appaloosa that never spotted. Later, Hank asked Dad to board Jimbo, a nice horse, which I believe brought in another $25 a month.

At first Mom was resistant; she didn't want a strange man and horse on our farm. As it turned out, Mr. Weinkauf was a nice man who owned a heating and air conditioning business in Racine. Because of his work schedule, he often came at odd times to do his chores. Sometimes he would bring along his three sons, who were scared to death of the horses.

Hank was the only one who could ride Black Jack. He often took him to the horse show down by Harmie's, at Highway 31 and Lichter Road. He would put Vick's Vapor Rub in the horse's nose so it wouldn't smell any female horses.

Hank sometimes helped with mechanical challenges we always seemed to have on our farm. Hank would pay Mark and me to do his chores when he and his family went on vacation. One night in Black Jack's stall, I was trying to get him to move over so I could put grain into his feed box. I was probably about thirteen. When he kicked me, it hurt so badly I was sure he had snapped my femur. I'm thankful he wasn't wearing horseshoes at the time, and that he didn't get me six inches farther north.

Looking back, I am amazed we ever had any horses to ride. Dad always hated feeding any livestock you couldn't either sell or eat.

The first horse I remember was Lady. When Mark was just three or four, he was riding Lady and she walked under a tree with low-hanging branches, which scraped him up pretty badly.

One snowy Christmas, Dad bought a buggy, which Lady pulled. He gave five or six of us kids a two-mile ride around the block. The buggy still hangs in the barn today.

Pokey was another horse we had for several years. She was gentle and we used to ride her bareback. Jane remembered, "She was always a lot more cooperative when she was heading back to the barn." When Pokey died, we dug a big hole and buried her on the west end of the woods. A big hole requires lots of digging.

One of Dad's dreams was to have a pair of draft horses. This dream never came about, maybe because we had eleven kids who all attended Catholic schools and extra money was never available.

Growing up we always had a female collie, a beautiful breed. They make great watchdogs and they don't bite. Dad always wanted a good litter of pups. Whenever the dog came into heat he would stick her up in the barn, to protect her from the neighborhood mutts.

Dad worked a lot of hours and never got our dog to a good sire. Plus, he didn't always get her to the haymow soon enough. Wouldn't you know that when collies had mongrel pups they always had ten or twelve pups in the litters.

Some farms have a disease called distemper. Snooky was the pup we lost to this killer. For a time, it wiped out our entire feline population as well. If dogs and cats are not vaccinated, they will die from the disease. I don't think most dairy farmers would ever invest the money it would take to treat two dozen farm cats. These were not pets. Why doesn't distemper kill any of the livestock on the farm? I always wondered about this.

I remember one of our collies got hit by a car on the road. After that, if our dog ever got to close to the highway, she got punished. We never again had problems with our dogs wandering across the road.

Dad believed Kelly was part border collie, because she was smaller than a normal collie and mostly black and white. She was my favorite dog, a great companion for many years. As a pup she got too close to the road, and Dad hit her with the hoe. She had a lump on her skull but never again went near the highway.

Dad told a story about his special dog, Scotty. In 1956, when he sold his milk herd and young stock, a group of heifers milled around inside a ring of potential buyers. The cattle got spooked, broke through the circle, and ran down the pasture. Scotty rounded them up and drove them back into the ring. Ignoring the cattle, some farmers offered Dad good money for Scotty, but she wasn't for sale. Dad's hope was that Scotty would one day have pups that he could sell as cow-dogs. Unfortunately, she never had any offspring.

When we were young, we had barn cats. Some of the cats were great mousers. I remember a brown-and-white cat whose calico kitten later became a great barn cat. We also had a huge cream-colored tomcat that was valuable killing rats when we cleaned out the temporary silo. In later years, they all died off due to distemper.

We never had cats in the house. To this day I'm not fond of cats. Dogs will always love you. A cat gives you attention only when it wants something. It reminds me of selfish people; I don't like them much, either.

For a while we raised rabbits. We bought cages cheap from one of the former mink farms. Back in the sixties there were four mink farms within a mile-and-a-half of our home. When the market went bad, they all eventually went out of business.

Mom used to get lettuce, one of the rabbits' favorite foods, from a Racine grocery store. Some of the rabbits would get loose and we would see various colored rabbits running free around the barn. To this day, domestic rabbits are one of my favorite animals.

My Uncle Freddy used to raise goats and other farmyard animals on his Kansasville hobby farm. My younger sister Donna always enjoyed visiting his menagerie. One year he gave her a baby goat that she named Sniffer. Sniffer was never penned and became very personable; she thought she was a dog.

In the backyard, Sniffer was the only witness when I gave Audrey her engagement ring on July 4, 1975. We were married the following May 29, 1976. Eventually Sniffer was bred and had a kid of her own. It was a sad day for Donna when the decision was made to part with them both. When Donna received the money she earned from the sale it eased her pain considerably.

When we were kids we always had bantam chickens called banties. They are probably two-thirds the size of most other chickens, pretty with many assorted colors, but mostly brown. We would raise up to ten broods each summer. It was fun watching a hen with her chicks scratching around the barnyard for food. Each hen would find a hiding place to lay her eggs. They always cackle when they lay an egg. When she thought she had enough she would sit on them until the eggs hatched.

Sometimes when cleaning out a haymow we would run into powdered green eggs left from the banties. That meant they were really old. The smell was awful. Have you ever heard the term madder than a wet or setting hen? A chicken trying to protect her eggs will always peck at an intruder. We kids would check the hens to see how many eggs they had. For a young kid having a setting hen peck you was scary, until you learned it didn't really hurt. For me, that was one of the hurdles I crossed while growing up.

In the winter months, we would butcher chickens on Saturday for Sunday dinner. Chickens roost after dark, so you selected which ones you wanted, then easily grabbed them by the legs off their perches. With an axe we chopped off their heads then watched them run and jump. You have to have seen them "Running around like a chicken with its head cut off" to fully appreciate the phrase. You always stayed far enough away so you didn't get sprayed with blood.

Next, we dressed the chickens. I don't know where that expression came from, because you did just the opposite. You held them by the feet, dipped them in boiling water, and then plucked them, pulling off all the feathers. You rinsed all the debris off the bird with clean water.

Next you cut them open from the bottom removing the rectum, intestines, heart, and lungs. You had to be careful not to rupture anything because you didn't want to contaminate the meat.

Then, you cut from the top to remove the neck and gizzard, which looks like a thick clam. From it, you removed the thick lining that held the grain. Some loved to eat the heart and gizzard of chickens. I wasn't one of them. We rinsed the meat well, let it soak in water overnight, and it was ready to cook the next day.

In later years, Dad brought in a coop and raised laying hens for their eggs. Fresh eggs always tasted better than store-bought.

Guinea hens are kind of a neat-looking bird, black with white spots. They are similar to a pheasant. I think they look like a small peacock without the tail or the colors.

Once Dad decided to get a pair of guinea hens. He thought it might be fun to have a pair on the farm. They make great watchdogs, as their squawking alerts you anytime someone arrives on your property. Legend says their screeching keeps rats away.

One pair soon became a dozen. When they roosted, the Guineas had droppings all over everything. They cried at anything that moved. By the end of summer, Dad had had enough of this experiment. We ate them that fall and winter and never raised Guinea hens again.

In later years, Dad raised mostly ducks and a few geese. He put a chicken house across the drive close to the notorious willow tree. This tree had brittle limbs, and climbing it presented risks of falling. Near the willow Dad cooped his ducks, geese, and turkeys. You will never touch anything as soft as a newborn gosling, or baby goose.

Mom always fixed duck for Dad's birthday because it was his favorite meal. The secret to eating duck is that it has to be served hot. Dad never got his fill of duck until he started raising them, when we ate it frequently.

Dad used to buy and raise one hundred to two hundred Muscovy ducks for the holiday season. These were the ugly ducks with the red around the eyes and beak. They didn't have much fat and were great eating. One time I was butchering a duck and didn't yet understand the correct way to hold the head on the chopping block. Mr. Weinkauf, who boarded his horses at our farm, offered to help. Hank held the beak down for me and when the ax struck, blood sprayed all over his pants.

I later learned the correct way to chop the head off a duck is to hold the legs and wings by the tips and the bird's natural reaction is to stretch out its neck, making a perfect target.

Ducks are harder to butcher than chickens because they have pinfeathers, which are difficult to remove by hand. Dad solved this problem by using a vat of melted wax. Once all the big feathers were plucked from the bird, we dipped it into the tub. The wax formed what looked like a cast around the bird. Once it cooled, we removed the cast and the pinfeathers came right out. The wax chunks were put in the vat, and when they melted, all the debris floated to the top. We then skimmed off the impurities, leaving clean wax for the next time. Eventually Dad hired someone to butcher his ducks. Mark and I were away at college when he decided he had too many to do alone. Good help was hard to find.

When the geese grew up, they made great watchdogs. They honked a lot and they went after intruders. It was said if they grabbed your finger or hand, they could break a person's wrist by shaking it. I don't know if that was true, and I was not willing to find out.

Dad sold a pair of geese to our neighbor, Jerry Jensen, and his two birds scared many people away. I found that if they came after you, just grab them by the neck. It was fun to watch them try to run. They are top-heavy and stumble all over themselves trying to escape. Oh, the little things that entertained us when we were young!

We never had turkeys when I was growing up. Dad had them later. They say that domestic turkeys, along with sheep, are the stupidest creatures ever to raise on a farm. Though Dad had much success with chickens and ducks, turkeys were a whole different experience. One time my brother-in-law got a dozen baby turkeys for Dad. All but two died. That Thanksgiving Dad said, "That was the most expensive turkey I have ever eaten." Eventually Dad figured out how to raise turkeys that survived until November. It was always a learning curve with animals on the farm.

Mom liked having a parakeet in the house, I guess because she enjoyed its chatter. When there wasn't a lot of traffic, Mom would open the cage door and let Trixie fly throughout the downstairs of the house. When she was ready for Trixie to return to the cage, we kids would capture her by throwing a sheer curtain over her. Having the parakeet fly free was fun, like having our own personal aviary. That worked until someone opened a door and the bird was gone. She wasn't trying to escape, just testing her wings. The problem was the bird didn't know how to get back in. We don't know how many times this happened. Once when Donna and Beth were young, Trixie flew away. Mom raced to town in search of her replacement. Her goal was to find the identical twin of the first one so that the girls wouldn't find out. Years later Donna and Beth claimed they knew.

Dad's Farm Equipment

Once Mark and I were only twelve and thirteen running Dad's farm machinery while Dad was at work. We had to run the silo filler with the belt powered by the International Farmall H, which we called the Big Tractor or the H. Then we pulled the wagons with either our John Deere A or our Allis-Chalmers cultivating tractor, the Little Tractor. This was always dirty, dusty work, but for boys entering our teens, it was always a thrill knowing we were successfully doing the work of grown men.

In 1948, Dad bought the H, a new 1947 International Farmall H four-cylinder model. Since its purchase, it has been overhauled and painted numerous times. How could Dad have known that besides the farm, the H was going to be the most important purchase he ever made. For years that International Farmall H was the backbone of our farming operation. It was used in making almost every other piece of farm equipment do its job.

In spring, the H pulled the manure spreader, plow, and disk and drag that turned and worked the soil. It was used for watering and pulling the various planters, as well as cultivating the crops. In summer and fall, this tractor was used in numerous ways to complete the harvest. In winter, the H was used to pull our cars through deep snow and to make them fire on those frigid mornings when they wanted to sleep.

Allis-Chalmers B
Cultivating Tractor.

One-bottom plow,
below, and
hay loader, right.

Dump Rake.

Farming used to be so physically intense, slow, and tedious. At one time a forty- to eighty-acre farm was the norm. Today, farms sometimes are thousands of acres. Farming today is performed with less than one percent of the physical effort required a hundred years ago.

Years ago, all cars, trucks, and tractors required a crank for starting, because electric starters had not yet been invented. Cranking a tractor was a dangerous task on the farm, because sometimes a crank broke an arm or a wrist. One time when we were kids, the crank slipped off the crankshaft, smashing Dad's face and causing the blood to flow freely. Before Dad would let Mom see his broken nose, and before making the necessary trip to the hospital, he first washed his face in the water tank in the milk house. I don't know how we ever kept track of that crank, because it would just sit on the floor of the tractor. It could have slid off anytime. One spring Dad did plow it under. For a whole year the crank sat fourteen inches under the ground. The following spring, we plowed it back up to the surface.

During the 1950s and 1960s, Wisconsin winters consisted of a lot of snow and sub-zero days. When we were growing up, I seldom heard Dad use bad language unless I was in the horse barn holding the light on a frigid day or night while Dad cussed the H. These were the times he had to use the tractor to get everything else moving. We didn't have a snowplow, so a tractor was sometimes required to pull the car from deep snow. Also, on cold mornings if the car didn't want to wake up, you got it running by spraying ether in the carburetor. If that didn't work, you pulled it with a log chain hooked to the tractor to pop the clutch. In the days of steel bumpers, the car wouldn't come apart. This is what it took to get the engine to fire, to start up.

I have one friend in Iowa who is both a veterinarian and a farmer. In the 1980s he was feeding a thousand cattle. Like my Dad, Eldon was always in a rush and usually short of help.

By himself he would operate two tractors at once. He would get the first tractor pulling forward, hop off, then jump on the second tractor, pop the clutch and hope it started.
OSHA laws don't deal with the self-employed, but OSHA officials would have fainted anyway. One frigid day it took longer than usual to get the second tractor started. His first tractor crashed into a steel grain bin.

Dad was never very mechanical, but the H was pretty simple and he could do most maintenance that was required to keep it running. We sometimes had to turn off the gas when we were done using it, so we wouldn't have a puddle of gas on the floor the next morning. Other times on a cold night we drained the radiator so it wouldn't freeze up when we didn't have the proper amount of antifreeze in the tractor.

Today the only job required of this semi-retired tractor is to pull the wagon for hayrides. My brother Mike still gives several hayrides at each of the family's many gatherings throughout the year. For years we used a hay wagon with bales of hay or straw as seats. In more recent years, we have used a trailer that is lower to the ground and much easier for people to get on and off. It has cushioned chairs for us older riders, and an old carpet on the floor making comfortable seating for the kids. Some family members and visitors to the farm enjoy the hayride so much they ride every time the wagon leaves the yard. The Thomas and Mueller family picnics always have more than one hundred in attendance. If the picnic is just our immediate family, brothers and sisters, their kids and grandchildren, we may number only seventy-five.

Most of our field cultivating was done two rows at a time with the International H. To cultivate our garden, though, we used a one-row cultivator attached to our orange Allis-Chalmers B tractor with wide front wheels. The cultivator was pretty important, because it meant we didn't have to hoe by hand all the weeds in our five acres of sweet corn. The Allis-Chalmers was fun to operate, when we could keep it running. It had a kind of bench seat much different from the International H or John Deere A. I remember we tried to make a homemade cover to shade us by bending re-rod and attaching cardboard to block the sun. If we had known back then how dangerous the sun's rays were, we probably would have purchased umbrellas and mounted them on all of our tractors.

The John Deere A was bigger than the Farmall H. It had a two-cylinder engine and was about the same age as the H. There was a hand clutch on the right, which was kind of touchy anytime you were trying to hook up a piece of equipment. Dad bought it to pull the plow and disk. As Dad used to say, "It has more guts," that is, more pulling power. I know this tractor had an electric starter, because I don't ever remember having to crank it.

When Dad was recovering from back surgery during the winter of 1966-1967, he may have saved Matt Keen's life. Matt was a neighbor and Dad's friend. It is a mystery how they could have gotten along so well; Dad was a diehard Democrat, and Matt was a conservative Republican. I guess that was okay, as long as Matt wasn't rich. They must not ever have talked politics. When Matt died in 1972, Dad said, "Liberal George McGovern's nomination for president that year must have been what killed him."

Matt was one of the first in our area to have electricity. He wired his barn before the house, because there were no cows to milk in the house. Matt had two sons, Jack and Pete, who were both single. They worked with their Dad operating his farm and helping with his custom farm work operation. They plowed, did field work, planted, and harvested for many local farmers each season. This was during the Vietnam War. Jack had been drafted and was already serving in the Army when Pete got his draft notice. Matt had a bad heart and wasn't going to be able to work without Pete. After Matt shared his predicament with my father, Dad contacted our Democratic Congressman's office to see what the options were. In order for Pete to get a deferment, Matt had to get a letter from each of his customers explaining how necessary Pete's services were to them. Because Dad was convalescing from his own major back surgery, he took the time to see each of Matt's customers and get the required paper work to keep Matt in business. After Jack returned, then Pete also honorably served his country. It was just another example of Dad demonstrating his Golden Rule philosophy.

To show his appreciation, in the spring of 1967 Matt brought over his two Case steel-wheeled tractors to plow our farm. The big back wheels on each tractor had three rows of spikes. These were the only steel-wheeled tractors I have ever seen actually working in the field. According to Dad, Matt was a mechanical genius and was able to keep the tractors in working order. Matt had a huge trailer to haul his tractors, unlike anything I had ever seen. The trailer bed angled down to the ground when he backed the tractors off. Then when he drove them back on, it rose to be level again. When my brother Mike was a senior in high school, he got to drive these tractors. They were hard to maneuver and required a lot of strength to operate, but I wish I had had the opportunity to run one of these classic antiques.

Another time Dad helped out Matt when Dad was asked to supply two cows for a milking competition at Johnson Wax Corporation. We had only one milk cow, a Guernsey. So Dad contacted Matt, who was paid pretty well to supply two Holstein cows for the event. The company had a milking contest between the foreign dignitaries and those from the U.S. It sounded like a lot of fun. The Americans at the company hadn't milked as many cows by hand, so they lost badly.

Each spring before planting, we kids picked rocks. I guess the winter frost and plowing the soil brought them to the surface of the fields. The rocks had to be removed before planting so they wouldn't damage the farm equipment. We owned a thick steel skid platform we pulled through the field with a tractor, over freshly worked ground. As kids, one of our jobs was to walk the field picking up rocks and pitching them onto the skid. If you cringe at nails on a chalkboard, you would have had real problems every time the steel scraped over a rock. Maybe that is why Jane to this day can't stand the scraping of silverware on glass plates. Later, Dad had a 1951 Chevy pickup with its floor rusted out of its box. He used steel from the skid to make a new floor for his truck bed. From that point, we drove the fields with the Chevy, pitching rocks into the bed as we walked. For years we had a big rock pile on the southeast corner of our woods. Not having any use for rocks, Dad gave most of them away to anyone who was building a house. Today people buy rock by the pound. We may have been sitting on a gold mine.

Dad had a one-bottom, walk-behind plow. I think it originally belonged to his cousin Norm. This implement was initially built to be pulled by a team of two draft horses. Dad used this plow to dig twelve-inch furrows when he planted his asparagus. Dad also owned a two-bottom plow that was pulled by our 1947 International Farmall H tractor. Each trip down the field turned a twenty-eight-inch swath of earth. At the end of each season we greased the plow blades, to keep them from rusting. The following year after the first pass through the field, the blades would shine like new. The dirt would slide right off.

In the age before no-till farming, fuel was cheap. Every farmer plowed, or turned over the soil, every year. Before chemicals were used for eliminating weeds and bugs, insects were killed each season by putting them several inches under the earth. The plow flipped the top fourteen inches of soil. Any plant debris was turned under and helped fertilize future crops. When farmers plowed in the fall, it was easier the next spring to break up the soil for planting. The only downfall was that sometimes erosion problems were created. After plowing, the ground was disked and dragged, usually with two passes required before the ground was smooth enough for planting. A drag was pulled behind the disk to level out the soil. The disk and drag were ten feet wide.

When a young boy was learning to drive a tractor, disking the field was one of the first tasks he was given. He had to be able to drive a straight line and pay attention to the equipment to make sure everything was working properly. Audrey's younger brother was once working the field and the big back wheel fell off the tractor. So much for being alert. It gave him a good scare and luckily, he wasn't hurt.

For putting in our sweet corn crop, Dad used a two-row corn planter. For each row, there was a covered metal container, called a box, for seed, and another for fertilizer. Under each seed box was a plate which dispensed seed into the ground. Each planter came with several different plate sizes that made it possible to plant other crops in addition to corn. The rotating back wheel of the planter metered how much fertilizer and seed were dropped. For corn, a kernel was planted every few inches. The machine had a marker that dug a line in the dirt, so the driver knew where to plant the next two rows. This made for straight rows the proper distance apart. Back then we planted thirty-six-inch rows, I believe. Perfect rows were important for aesthetics, but also so emerging crops could be cultivated properly. Originally, rows were determined by the width of the draft horse pulling the implements, forty inches, I think.

Dad used a cabbage planter for planting strawberries and tomatoes. This machine had a thirty-gallon water tank on the back, along with two seats eight inches off the ground. Two people sat on the planter, one on each side of the row being planted. Every couple of feet the machine dug a four- or five-inch furrow. The riders sat with plants on their laps and took turns reaching down to insert a plant into the trench. One person used his left hand and the other used his right. After each plant was put in the ground, water drained into the hole, and another shovel spread dirt around the roots of the newly planted strawberry or tomato plant. By the time Tim started working summer jobs and then later left for college, Mom and Dad's truck garden was a busy eight-acre enterprise. Donna recalls that she and Beth helped Dad plant tomatoes. They are both left-handed and could never figure out the sequence on the cabbage planter. They would get laughing so hard they would miss most of the holes. Dad didn't appreciate having to go back and re-plant by hand. That defeated the purpose of why he used the planter in the first place. Dad's solution was to have Donna drive the tractor. The crop all got planted, but the rows were never very straight. Straight rows were a priority for all good farmers.

Corn binders were originally pulled by horses before tractors and choppers were invented, and later outfitted to be pulled by tractors. A binder cut the corn stalks at the ground then bundled them. The binder carried a small bale of twine. Each bundle was tied before being dropped from the machine. These were then either shocked, that is, stood in a pile which resembled a small teepee, or put onto a wagon to be carried to the silo and made into silage.

Several summers we made sweet corn silage for our cattle to eat the following winter. As soon as we were finished picking each field, we made silage as soon as possible, because green stalks had the most food value and flavor. The silo filler was a machine that chopped the green corn stalk bundles into silage, which made it easier for the cows to eat. The filler was powered by a belt that ran from the tractor. We fed the corn bundles into the silo filler to grind the stalks into silage, then blew it up into the temporary silo we made on the concrete barn floor with snow fencing. We added a thick waterproof paper inside the snow fence. The paper kept the silage airtight as it fermented and prevented silage from spoiling. It was fun making this antique equipment work for our purposes. Binders and silo fillers had first been used decades before we were born. Our silo would reach fifteen feet in height with a diameter of eight to ten feet. This would produce enough food for our milk cow and eight growing calves and last until the following spring. Making sweet corn silage was one of our favorite chores. It was neat to see our homemade silo grow toward the barn's roof. The cow and calves loved this sweet feed, and it was a lot less boring than just feeding dry ground feed. We also used the silo filler for chopping old hay for mulching our raspberries in the spring. It operated by a belt from the H. It is amazing we were running this equipment by twelve years old. Look at the lessons we were able to learn at such a young age.

Today combines pick and shell the field corn, and then it is stored in grain bins. When we were kids, corn was picked on the ear and stored in corncribs so that circulating air would keep the corn dry, preventing it from spoiling. Corn pickers were either mounted right onto the tractor or pulled behind. Ours was a single-row picker that we pulled with the tractor. The picker pulled a hay wagon with sides to catch the ears of corn as each ear dropped from the chute above. Our corncrib was behind the barn. The big problem with corncribs was that they created havens for rats that fed off the corn.

Dad thought it was important to own a mechanical manure spreader, which had a drive wheel that moved the bars in the bed of the spreader. These bars moved the manure to the back, where rotating bars threw the manure into the field behind. As a young man, Dad had worked for a tightwad neighbor. Dad shared the story of spreading manure using a hay wagon, pitching it onto the wagon and off with a pitchfork. When Dad asked the neighbor why he didn't purchase a modern spreader like everyone else, his response was, "The wheels pack the soil too much." The real reason was that during the Depression, the neighbor could always hire a neighborhood kid to do it for minimal wages.

You never wanted to spread manure on a windy day. If you had to, it was important that the spreading mechanism was engaged only when you were driving upwind. Otherwise, you were covered with manure and weren't going to be allowed in the house until you stripped down to your underwear. You spread manure only when the ground was dry or frozen or else otherwise you would sink the tractor and spreader in the mud. Because we didn't have a lot of livestock, we could wait until it was dry in the spring to spread manure before we planted. Our spreader had a sliding tongue. This made it easy to hook up to the tractor. Then when the tractor pulled forward, the bar slid into place, bringing the spreader up off the ground. When you unhooked you pulled the lever forward and backed up to take the weight off the tractor, making it easy to unhook.

In the spring of 1966 we were sorting lumber in the horse barn. We used the spreader to haul the scraps to the burn pile. The tongue mechanism wasn't working properly, so Dad tried to lift the front of the spreader that weighed several hundred pounds. He crushed three discs in his back, and he was in great pain and laid up for months. Eventually he had back surgery. The doctor decided that because Dad was too old at forty-eight, he wasn't going to fuse the discs. He just removed the bad ones. Dad never again worked as a cement finisher, which required constant bending. Instead he worked several years as a construction laborer before his retirement at age sixty-two.

A dump rake was the predecessor to the modern hay rake that windrows hay before baling. These rakes had long tines that would drag the cut hay until it was in a pile. These were used before hay balers, when hay was put into barns loose. It probably required ten times the labor of hay bales.

The rotary hoe was the most fun piece of equipment to operate. It was about eight feet wide. We pulled it through the field with the tractor in road gear, about twenty miles per hour. The rotary hoe was used after the new soybean plants popped through the soil. We ran the tractor wheels between the rows of soybeans. The hoe had many spiked wheels that popped the surface dirt around the plants so all the new growth of weeds would lie on top of the dirt, dry up, and die.

When we were kids Dad had a slusher. It looked like a wheelbarrow with handles in the back, but without a wheel. Flat on the bottom, slushers were pulled with a chain by horses and then later by a tractor. Before modern excavating equipment these were used for digging basements. A farmer would plow the area where a house was going to be built. Using a slusher was a two-man job. One person would drive a team of horses, then another person would walk behind the slusher, getting it in position to dig with it. The slusher would haul all the loose dirt and rocks away from the area so a basement could be built for a house. By pulling up on the handles, the operator scooped up the loose dirt. When it was full, he would push down on the handles and the slusher would skid across the earth. When the worker was ready to dump, he lifted the handles and the slusher would empty just like a wheelbarrow. Each time all the overturned soil was removed, the horses and plow would dig down another twelve inches to loosen the dirt for the slusher. Digging a basement took days or weeks. Today with a backhoe, a basement can be dug in a couple of hours.

Dad, like his father, would lend anything he had to others if they needed it. Apparently, our slusher was borrowed and never brought back. Dad didn't know what became of it. I haven't seen it since my early teens.

Vehicles

In high school, Mark and I owned a black 175cc Kawasaki motorcycle that was always breaking down. I think it had a wiring problem. This is the bike Mark and I took on the trip to Devil's Lake. It is amazing we ever made it. Our second bike we bought during college. It was a 350cc Honda. The body was metal flake bronze color. It got much use. We took turns using it for work in the summer. During the school year, Mark kept it at his fraternity house at Platteville. I was dating Audrey, so when the weather was nice we would use it a lot on weekends. These small bikes were not made for traveling. Whenever Audrey and I rode, frequent stops were necessary. These delays always tested my patience. One time on a trip from Janesville to Kenosha, she couldn't breathe very well because she had a bad cold, plus the seat vibration was painful. It was a long sixty miles that day. From a friend Dad bought a 1956 Chevy real cheap. It was calico in color with two shades of blue and primer brown. Someone had started to repair the body but never finished. Mark and I drove that our senior year, and then Jane drove it after we went off to college.

My earliest memories of our family cars include a green Nash and then a blue Nash, both with wing windows at the front to give us a breeze. That was before air conditioning. The little window in the back had a screen. When we went to the drive-in theater after dark, we could get some air without being eaten by mosquitoes. For years, we had station wagons to better haul our whole crew. The first one was a 1960 blue vehicle with a white stripe on the side. It had a bench seat for both the back and front seat; both held several kids.

We had a pink, originally red, 1951 Chevy pickup truck with big fenders on front and back and a spotlight. We used to ride its neat running

Above, Dad with the Rambler station wagon that hauled pigs and calves in addition to kids. Left, Bill on his 350 Honda on one of his motorcycle trips during college. Below, Dad with a load of firewood for Mark's business, with one of the collies. The pump house is in the background.

boards when we ran it in the garden or field. Looking at the size of trucks today, it doesn't seem that it could have been too practical, but it was a lot of fun. The box in the back was tiny, and the cab sat only two people comfortably. We used this truck to pick up bales of hay. Fully loaded, it could hold about twenty bales.

When Tom left for the Army in January 1970, he left his 1960 or 1962 big old beige Dodge with no reverse. Instead of a shifter, it had push buttons on the dash. I used it to go to work that summer at the A&W root beer stand. We had a 1964 green-and-white La Saber sedan that was in pretty good shape and fun to drive. I remember it had a button to set the maximum speed. If you exceeded it, an alarm would go off. In those days the speed on a two-lane highway was 65 miles per hour; at night it went to 55 miles per hour.

About 1970, Dad bought a grass-green pickup. It was a heavy brute that after using for some time we learned had no back brakes. A couple of years later when Mark and I were seniors, Dad bought a 1967 baby blue Chevy pickup. We were delighted. It was a nice truck that was used for many farm and family chores. The spring of our freshman year Mark and I were home, I think over Easter. At the last minute our ride fell through so we brought the truck back to school. It was kind of neat taking a road trip in our pickup truck.

Garden Produce: A Family Affair

Mom and Dad got serious about truck gardening in the early 1960s, I suppose when we kids got old enough to help. In the early years, Dad put most of our garden on the west end of the woods where our best soil was. It was a quarter-mile from the house and a jaunt for us kids to get to it. Because Dad worked so much, it was hard for him to supervise the cultivating and weeding that were necessary to harvest a good crop. He would get frustrated, because in those early years just about the only things he succeeded in raising besides kids were sweet corn and raspberries. Once we moved our garden north of the house, we began to raise a good variety of produce for sale.

Mom supervised the harvesting and sale of every bushel of tomatoes, apples, and cucumbers. We sold two hundred to three hundred gallons of cider, along with hay wagons of melons, squash, pumpkins, gourds, and Indian corn. We left school early only if a frost was coming and everything had to be picked before dark. Mom was always trying to figure where to get the most customer traffic. Aunt Jeanie, Mom's younger sister,

41

and Uncle Johnny Murphy lived at the intersection of Wood Road and Berryville Road on the edge of Kenosha, about a half-mile north of where Mom grew up, and now next to the University of Wisconsin-Parkside campus. Mom believed Aunt Jeanie's corner was perfect for marketing sweet corn. It had good traffic coming and going from Racine, plus it had a stop sign which gave people time to think about whether they wanted to make a purchase or not. Plus, my cousin Jerry, Jeanie's son, was a natural born hawker. He could sell anything knowing he was going to get ten percent of the purse. He sold on their corner for a number of years with great enthusiasm and success. When he got older and moved on to other opportunities, sales declined. His younger siblings weren't too interested in earning ten percent of their efforts.

Mom reluctantly set up a stand on our farm. Highway 31 was a much busier road, but with no stop signs. It was the main highway connecting Racine and Kenosha. Once customers became familiar with our stand, though, it turned out to be a great spot for selling throughout the next twenty years.

Sweet corn was our main crop. Multiple plantings on five acres meant we always had fresh corn from mid-July through Labor Day. We always had early maturing corn, because customers were looking for it in July. It was never as good; the ears were smaller with less flavor. One year, Dad planted sweet corn on March 23. It froze off, but he was willing to take the risk because it would have sold for a high price. Also, there is a sense of victory when you are the first to have it. Our later maturing corn was Iowa Chief sweet corn. In the 1960s it was the best corn available, with its great flavor and huge ears.

In the early 1960s, sometimes we were picking before sunrise to have the corn to the grocery store in Racine before 7 a.m. We sold it for a half-cent an ear. On the roadside, it sold for twenty-five cents a baker's dozen. If the corn wasn't picked that day, or had a worm in the end, we didn't sell it. Our family always got the short ears after the wormy end had been broken off. The cows and hogs got the day-old stuff. Mom, the chief picker, had us at a young age drag corn in gunnysacks back to our Rambler station wagon. The number of ears we toted depended on how big we were. Older helpers became assistant pickers, but it was a serious sin to open an ear before picking or to pick an ear not yet ripe. Either was not sellable. On Sundays we used to sell more than one hundred dozen. It was always a baker's dozen with thirteen ears.

One year we planted corn down by the creek. We had a lot of rain and we waded through several inches of water to pick the crop. During football practice our freshman year, I developed an allergic reaction. My face swelled up like a marshmallow. We never knew for sure, but we suspected that the corn was the culprit. That is funny because by then, I had been dragging or picking sweet corn much of my life. I know my brothers and sisters weren't very happy that the patch became off limits for me from then on.

Every spring, Dad would clean the raspberries by pulling out all the dead shoots from the previous year and trimming the new about knee high. I don't know when he found time. I remember when we had seven rows of raspberries from the end of Uncle Sam's flower garden, which covered probably a third of an acre, north from Grandma's trailer for probably one hundred feet. Then our raspberries went all the way to the woods. Whenever we had hay or straw that was damaged by the rain before it was safely baled, we would pile it on the southeast side of our seven-acre woods. It would sit until the following year. Then during our spring break from school, we would run it through our old silo filler onto our hay wagons. From there we sprinkled it on the raspberries as mulch. This helped the plants hold moisture during the hot dry summer and prevented weeds from competing with the crop. The old hay also allowed a berry picker's feet to stay clean and safe from the mud caused whenever it rained.

Raspberries were our second biggest crop after sweet corn. In June, when the raspberries were ripe, we usually picked and sold more than a thousand pints most summers. One season after Audrey and I were married, the rain cooperated, and the patch produced an amazing two thousand pints. We used some wood pint boxes, but most were plastic. When using the plastic, we had to put raspberry leaves in the bottom so the berries wouldn't fall through the holes.

Not everyone was let into the raspberry patch to pick, because inexperienced pickers would cost Mom and Dad money. Good pickers moved the bushes around so they could see all the fruit. They were gentle so the raspberries would not get knocked to the ground. Slow pickers either didn't have a good eye, knocked too many berries on the ground, or were eating too many. When spotted, they were given a tutorial, but if they didn't improve, they were banned from the patch and given other chores. Dad and we boys all learned to pick, but over the seasons most of the crop each year was picked by Mom and her sisters, my sisters, and Steve. We each were assigned positions to pick in. There were pickers on each side of the row across from each other. The best pickers were always given the best spots, because they didn't miss any berries and they worked faster.

We picked every couple of days during a raspberry season that lasted probably three weeks.

We had strawberries growing up, but they were not our big money crop like sweet corn and raspberries. Mom grew up on a strawberry farm, so maybe that was why she chose not to make strawberries our big cash crop. Her Dad, Grandpa George Thomas, raised three acres of strawberries he sold in Chicago, where he made good money. His was a more labor-intensive crop than what we had. Grandpa had fourteen kids, so I'm sure they all became well acquainted with strawberries. Strawberries, like raspberries, always took a couple of years to start producing. In the spring we mulched them during our Easter break.

We had a Whitney crabapple tree by the driveway. It was an early apple, small and sweet, great for kids. Some years that tree would be loaded. We used to hold our shirts out in front of us and load up with apples when we went to bale hay or straw in August. If an orchard owner wanted to have nice bug-free apples in the fall, it was required to spray the trees once in early spring with a dormant spray and then several times during the summer. Mr. Holy, Chuck Hartig's grandfather, lived across the road and had a small orchard of his own. For years, he sprayed Dad's trees using a thirty-gallon sprayer that he pulled with his little tractor. On windy days, Mr. Holy would finish covered with insect poison. Spraying always made Dad nervous. Even back in the 1950s, he knew chemicals were dangerous. Not surprisingly, Mr. Holy died of cancer a few years later. A farmer friend said, "If you can't hold it in your hands, it's not safe." When I was young, our apple orchard had twenty or twenty-five trees with many varieties. Some that I remember were Transparent, Greening, Dutchess, Snow Apple, Jonathan, McIntosh, Red Delicious, Rome Beauty, Yellow Delicious, and Russet.

The Garden of Eden wasn't the only place where hanging apples were tempting. For young kids on the farm, they were great ammunition for anyone contemplating an apple fight with siblings or friends. Because apples were such a valuable commodity, Dad would really get angry if he knew we were picking apples before they were ripe.

Our trees were more than twenty feet tall. The best apples often were at the far end of the limbs, which made them difficult to reach. Dad had two huge, rickety ten-foot picking ladders. We stood on these to pick everything on the outside of the tree. Anything too high for the ladders or on the inside we climbed the limbs to get. When picking we wore canvas apple picker bags to hold the apples. These could be adjusted to hold either a half or three-quarters of a bushel. They had shoulder and waist straps, so the bag would hang in front of our waist. Both hands then would be free to pick the apples, unless we were high in the tree and needed one wing to prevent ourselves from falling to the ground.

High in the tree, we sometimes had thirty pounds of apples hanging precariously from our midsection. When the bag got full, we would unbuckle our shoulder harness and lower it six or eight feet for someone below to empty into a bushel basket. Apple-picking season was great fun for us kids. We learned to climb and lost much of our fear of heights at the same time. Naturally, Mom always encouraged us to be careful while in the trees. Uncle Sam, Dad's older brother, lived in the trailer with Grandma. One season, while picking apples he fell from a ladder, breaking his collarbone. We shook the limbs of the tree to bring down all the apples that we couldn't reach while picking. These windfalls were mostly used for making cider, and a few Grandma would make into applesauce. We often gave apples to the nuns in Racine. Sometimes they would even come out to our farm to pick. We sold our apples at our roadside stand by the bushel, half-bushel or three-pound bag. Some we saved for our family's use during the winter. With eleven kids we used to eat a bushel of apples a week. To this day, apples are still one of my favorite foods.

We got a good apple crop every other year. In those years, we made cider three or four times in the fall. It was labor-intensive, taking many hours to prepare the apples, clean the jugs, and bottle the cider afterward. Apple cider was never a moneymaker, but most of us just enjoyed the process anyway. After school in the evenings we used gunnysacks to pick up our windfall apples, leaving the rotten ones on the ground. We put them in a tank of water, sorting them a second time. The bad ones were pitched, and the good ones were wiped off and re-bagged for the trip to the cider mill. Mom used to buy one-gallon glass jugs from the local 7-Up bottler. These jugs had contained the syrup which was used to make soda. Washing out every bottle was tedious work but was necessary each time we made cider.

As cider ages, it becomes alcohol. Once in the early years, a gallon of working cider exploded in Uncle Leo's Union Grove basement. To prevent any further accidents, we always removed the cardboard cork from inside the metal cover for each bottle.

When we were young, we used to have cider made on Highway U in Oak Creek, always on Friday nights. We would make fifty to seventy gallons each trip, totaling two to three hundred gallons a season. When we had real juicy apples, we would get three gallons from every bushel. Normally it was two-and-a-half gallons. Based on the number of apples we had, we knew how much cider would be produced each time. Because I was too young to unload gunnysacks or wrestle milk cans, I don't recall much about the actual making of the cider. I do remember that we dumped the apples on an elevator that took them up into the haymow. Then, when the process was complete, we took our cider home.

The farm where we pressed our apples into cider had a big yard, so while we waited we played football and other yard games. In the fall, with the shorter days, our games always ended in the dark, which was kind of scary for this little kid.

We tried to get to the cider mill early so we didn't have to wait in line behind three or four other customers. For sure, we always wanted to be ahead of the guy whose orchard was in a goose pasture. His dirty apple cider had a distinct taste.

Dad owned several seven-gallon milk cans. This is how we hauled our cider home from the mill. He didn't own any of the ten-gallon cans; when full, these were too heavy for kids to handle. Friday night or Saturday morning we bottled our cider on the front porch. Using a thin cloth, we strained the cider from one milk can to another. With pans the juice was poured into the jugs. We had a unique funnel from an old coffee maker that held about a half-gallon at the top and had a straight shaft which fit perfectly into each bottle for filling. After the foam settled, we topped off the jugs. During the bottling process, we always had the hose running to keep everything from becoming sticky and to keep the sweat bees at bay.

In the late 1960s and early 1970s, we went to the Uhlenhake farm on Highway 43 in Kenosha on Saturday mornings to have our cider made. By this time, we boys could make the trip by ourselves. Their press was in an old dairy milk house. They used a hammermill for crushing the apples. Farmers used to use these years earlier for grinding their livestock feed. This mill had a big bin on top to pour in the apples. Underneath was a big galvanized wash tub for catching the mash.

Except for the grinding of the apples, everything at this mill was done by hand. They had a four-foot-square table with a huge galvanized pan. Into this pan were set layers of mash with burlap in between. These layers were pressed into cider.

In later years, Dad used to plant one thousand tomato plants with the old cabbage planter. In August, our family would pick as many we could, then would allow people to come in and pick their own. One hot dry summer, when Audrey and I were either dating or first married, we spent a lot of time watering tomato plants. We had several fifty-five-gallon drums in the pickup truck, filled with water. Using siphon hoses, we watered every plant in the garden.

Our farm's soil was mostly clay and sand that was great for growing muskmelons. We sometimes picked melons by the pickup load. Muskmelons are easy to pick. When they are ripe, they have a yellow color and the stem pops right off. We did raise some watermelons but without the same success, because they need warmer temperatures.

My friend John McLean was a new Loras College graduate when he attended my sister Jane's wedding in June of 1977. He was from the south side of Chicago and had never spent time in a garden or on a farm. He didn't understand rain and its effects on travel when you're not using hard roads. Saturday during the night we got a pretty good rain. Before leaving for home the next morning in his father's new car, John decided to say goodbye to our Dad, who was working in the garden. When he saw Dad waving his arms and shouting, he thought Dad was just happy to see him. John got down the driveway okay, but when he turned into the field he didn't make it twenty feet. The car was buried axle-deep in the mud. With a chain hooked to the car's bumper, and our International H tractor, Dad was able to pull him to safety. Too bad John didn't have any help explaining to his father, also a city person, the concept of rain and mud in rural Wisconsin.

We sold fruits and vegetables all summer at Mom's produce stand, top right. Top left, Audrey waters tomato plants. Middle, Dad supervises watering with Mark at the truck and another person helping. Middle left, Bill pours cider from a milk can through a strainer held by Audrey. Left, Dad uses some of his cement finishing skills as he redoes the floor of the only bathroom in our old farmhouse. Dad worked as a cement finisher in construction for many years.

Chapter 3: Making Ends Meet

Dad worked jobs off the farm as his primary source of income. All else was supplemental income to providing for our large family. Everyone contributed in whatever way possible. Each child had responsibilities in the house, barn, or garden. Besides helping at home, Mark and I worked many jobs together, including working for our neighbors Mr. Wirtz, Mert Fink, and Ray Lichter. We also had jobs at a Christmas tree farm, a mink farm, a gas station, and worked on a ship docked on Lake Michigan.

Dad graduated from high school in 1936 during the Depression. Jobs were scarce, so he worked for local farmers for little pay until he was twenty-one in August 1940. He got a job at Lakeside Malleable Castings Company in Racine. Dad worked there for a year-and-a-half until he was drafted into the Army. Because this foundry was making war materials, Dad could have been deferred from the draft. Being a young guy looking for some action, he chose not to tell his boss about his draft notice. His boss was not happy losing a good employee when he learned Dad had only a few days until his departure.

When Dad returned from World War II four-and-a-half years later, his military service gave him more than five years of seniority. He chose to return to the foundry and partner with Larry Rashleger to do piecework. The foundry paid by piecework, thus an employee's income was based on how difficult a part was to complete and the number of parts the employee made. Dad and Larry lifted the moldings by hand, including a part that weighed in at three hundred twenty pounds. It took one year for them to perfect a system for making gray-iron castings. The following seven years they were the most productive and best-paid team in the foundry. Dad and Larry were never docked for mistakes. Their income was twice that of all other production workers. They became life-long friends.

The big bosses used to come to the foundry to see what Dad and Larry would charge to make a new part. After experimenting for a couple of days they would determine a price. Their price was always accepted. After ten years Dad started coughing up colored phlegm. His doctor said if he wanted to live to an old age, he had better find other work. He did and lived to be ninety-nine. Larry has been dead more than twenty years.

Larry was always so nice to us kids. He was a jack-of-all-trades who could fix, install, or build anything. When our coal furnace blew up about 1970, he put in a new natural gas one for Dad.

In February of 1954 or 1955, Dad quit the foundry and went right to work for Herb DeGrand, a neighbor who was a contractor. Herb taught him how to finish concrete. After completing just eight months of finishing cement, Dad switched jobs and went to work for American Motors Corporation as an inspector. In 1954, Nash Rambler, a division of Nash-Kelvinator Company, merged with Hudson Motor Car Company and became American Motors Corporation (AMC). My Uncle John Yacukowicz, who was married to Mom's younger sister Alice, had an important position at AMC.

According to Dad, when he talked about working at AMC, "It was the easiest job of my life." He made trips twice a day to Delavan to inspect cars after they were completed. Dad worked for American Motors for almost ten years. In 1963, AMC went on strike. With nine kids to support, Dad had no idea how long he would be without work. At the time, construction projects were prospering and paying good wages. Dad visited some of his former construction friends and decided to once again switch careers. He joined the union and was grandfathered in as a journeyman cement finisher. Because he was so particular about his finished product, he was kept working consistently.

After Dad injured his back in the spring of 1966 trying to lift the spreader hitch to hook it to the tractor, he ended up in the hospital with three crushed discs. A few days later, it was time for Beth to be born. With Dad in the hospital, Mom did not have a ride to the hospital, so she called Mike home from his high school prom. Still wearing his tuxedo, which made him look like a bridegroom on his wedding day, Mike, a high school junior, accompanied Mom to the maternity ward. I'm sure that onlookers immediately thought, That's cutting it close! While Mike was in the waiting room, an expectant father saw him and thought he looked pretty young. The father asked, "Is this your first?" and Mike answered, "No, this is No. 11!"

For three months, Dad was in horrible pain, thinking he was going to die. His first attempt to get relief was to see a chiropractor. When this lady wasn't able to improve the three crushed discs in his back, she should have sent him to an orthopedic surgeon. It was unfortunate that this incompetent practitioner hurt the reputation of her honorable profession. Dad eventually had back surgery. Normally, this surgeon would have fused the discs, but because of Dad's age, almost forty-eight, the surgeon chose to remove the discs instead. After his recovery, Dad went back to work on construction, but as a laborer, where he wouldn't be doing the necessary bending of a cement finisher. Dad never again had any major problems with his back.

I remember sometimes Mom would have to take Dad to work. She would be wearing her pajamas and a robe. Dad would get so irritated thinking her car would break down and she would be caught in her PJs.

In 1975 Dad decided to go back to AMC, thinking it would improve his retirement income. When he discovered it didn't, Dad went back and finished his career in construction. He retired in the fall of 1980 when he turned sixty-two. Maybe he saw the writing on the wall. In 1987, Chrysler acquired AMC so they could own Jeep, the most recognized vehicle in the world. Shortly after, AMC stopped building cars in Kenosha.

In construction, once lumber is no longer needed at a job site it is usually disposed of. Anytime the wood was still good, Dad's boss would let him bring it home. When I was a kid, we had plenty of lumber stored in our horse barn, mostly three-quarter-inch plywood and two-by-fours. This was the material construction workers used to pour concrete. For us kids this was great, because we usually had some sort of building project going on. We used the lumber to build a tree fort on our six acres across the road in the woods. These cast-offs also helped us fix up the old cabin and later build our coop for our racing pigeons.

Take a look in my garage today, and you'll see a supply of boards that have been saved from being burned or from other people's garages as they cleaned out spaces. Audrey and I have built headboards and complete beds for our grandchildren and many more projects from our stash of lumber.

Chores on the Farm

In the mid-1960s, Mom decided it was time to paint the barn. Somewhere they bought some cheap Army-green surplus paint, probably left over from World War II. This was used as primer for the first coat. The second coat was barn red. Both colors were oil-based. It was a mess to use and clean up. Gas would do the trick but that really wasn't the best for your skin. Tom and Mike were in high school at the time; I'm pretty sure they did most of the work, because Dad was always working his job or at home doing the necessary farm chores. We started with the front and sides, because that is what could be seen from the road. It did look pretty sharp upon completion. Mom was the driving force behind this project, so I'm pretty sure that is why at least three sides got done. This is what the neighbors could see. The front of the barn faced Highway 31 to the east, and the back walls were each twenty-five feet into the air. North and south walls under the peak of the barn reached thirty-five feet. All the painting was done from ladders. Quite a feat for teenage boys. We never did complete the back side. For years it remained Army green, until the barn blew down in a shear wind in the mid-1990s.

I guess we can be thankful our push mowers had gasoline engines and weren't the reel type. We were able to keep them running because fifty yards from our southern property line was a lawnmower repair business. It was just beyond "the restaurant," our family's nickname for the Country Kitchen next door. Some years we mowed part of the orchard, which increased our work from one to two acres of grass.

In our cow barn, the manure gutters were right behind where the cows stood stanchioned. The gutters were about four feet from both the east and west walls of the building. This created a walkway that we used to let the cow and calves out to pasture. We also used this aisle to wheel out manure whenever we cleaned the gutters behind the cows or cleaned calf pens. In the barn, a wheelbarrow was the most advanced piece of machinery that we used. Besides milking the cow and feeding all the livestock, chores included bedding the cattle. We shook straw underneath the cow and into the calf pens. This created a bed so the cattle stayed warm and dry and kept them off the uncomfortable concrete. In late winter or early spring, we used to clean the calf pens and the pigpen.

Sometimes that manure under the cattle was two feet deep. It would have been even deeper if the calves hadn't spent months tamping it down. The secret to cleaning barns was learning how to use a manure fork and removing the manure and straw mixture in layers. Each time the wheelbarrow was full, we took turns wheeling it out to the manure pile outside. We always wheeled across the top of a plank or series of planks to dump the manure on the far side of the pile we created. If you didn't quickly learn the fine art of pushing a wheelbarrow, you were soon re-scooping everything you had just spilled on the way. Hint: walk fast and learn to balance your load.

We always listened to 1960s music on the radio whenever we cleaned the barns. Regardless of how efficient we became, it still took hours to finish this task. Today whenever I have a job requiring a lot of concentration I prefer it be quiet. Maybe subconsciously music brings back these long-ago Saturdays, making it harder for me to think. When the fields became dry enough we loaded the manure spreader and spent days getting rid of our mounds of manure to the south and west of the barn. We parked the manure spreader, sometimes called a honey wagon, next to the barn, removed the west window, then pitched right through the opening. Pig manure is soupier than cow manure, because there is almost no straw in it. We avoided cleaning the pigpen on windy days, or else the manure would spray back into our face.

One summer Dad decided we were going to plant sugar beets to feed our cattle. He thought the beets would be a good food source for our milk cow and growing calves. We had an acre or two across the creek that wasn't being used. It was a couple of acres that had been in grass for quite a few years. We plowed and tilled the soil. Then using a dump rake, we pulled up all the dead quack grass roots to the surface. Once these were dry, we raked them into rows and then burned them. They burned well because of all the oil in the roots. The idea was by killing all the roots, the grass wasn't going to regrow and harm the growing sugar beets. This was back before the popular chemical Roundup. We then planted the field in sugar beets. We grew sugar beets two seasons. The first year the skin of the beet was red. The second year it went to more of an orange skin, and these were bigger, probably five pounds each. Sugar beets grow underground. I don't remember much about the harvest. I know it was hard work, because that's how we accomplished almost every job on our farm. We used a cleaver to chop the beets every night during chores. The cows loved them. It all ended, though, when Mom's milk customers complained that the beets affected the taste of the milk.

The key to building or putting up a fence was making it straight. We started by putting in the wood corner end post. These gave the fence the support it needed to stand strong. Wooden posts were placed at each corner or wherever the fence direction changed. Using a hand crank posthole digger, we dug a three-foot hole for each beam. These beams were stood upright in the hole, then dirt was packed around them to make them stable. Once these were set in place, the rest of the fence was built using steel posts. To make a straight fence, we had to learn how to eyeball a straight line between the corner post on each end. This task was impossible without two or more people. We drove the steel posts into the ground using a post driver, a steel cylinder that fit over the top of the post. It had a ten-pound weight welded to the top. We slammed this weight on top of the steel post over and over until it was driven to the desired height.

The electric wire was attached to insulators, two of which were tied to each post. These insulators kept the current flowing. To avoid electric shocks, livestock soon learned not to touch the fence. This juice is what keeps cows from getting out. Electric fences are designed to burn off any growing grass on a fence-line that touches the hot wire. It works great when the grass is dry. Keeping the wire hot is a big challenge for any farmer who uses electric fencing. Long wet grass, limbs, or debris can all short out a fence. Dad used to call his all-black Angus-Holstein cross calves Black Bastards. They were always the most curious and were the first to know when the fence wasn't working. Usually this was after a rain when the growing grass would fall on the wire, shorting out the fence.

Every kid who has grown up on a farm with assorted livestock and pasture knows the "joy" of a midnight hunt for black cattle in the fog or the pitch of night. For us it was along a busy Highway 31, usually in a wet eight-foot maze of corn. Maybe you have also been given the assignment of flagging down roaring eighteen-wheelers before they collided with your lost livestock. The following day we had to walk the whole fence looking for short circuits. This was a wet half-mile, and not much fun. One summer Mark and I came up with this brilliant idea for keeping the grass off the fence. We used Dad's one-bottom plow to plow a furrow, which covered the problem grass under the fence line. Unwittingly we created a greater problem. Once the new grass grew out of this new mound of soil, it now only had to grow half as tall to short out the fence.

When Mark and I were thirteen and fourteen, we decided to take the fence all the way down the lane and across the creek. It had been years since some of it had been used. In fact, that was the summer I learned that our farm on the southwest side was a couple of acres larger than I had realized. This was hard work cutting out years of underbrush and doing battle with the Brown Thrush mother birds that didn't want their sanctuary disturbed. It was pretty exciting seeing our cattle learning to cross the creek for the first time, and then exploring this new pasture.

For years we bought barley from a guy who lived south of Milwaukee. He worked for one of the Milwaukee breweries, and he used to clean up all the spilled barley, bring it home, and sell it cheap. Sometimes the grain was real clean and malted. The cows loved that. Other times it would be full of chaff or nuts, bolts, and nails. Dad bought a fanning mill, a machine that cleaned the barley, removing all the metal before it destroyed Dad's hammer mill. In the beginning we didn't have a pickup truck. We would bag the barley into gunnysacks and bring home a full load in the back of our Rambler station wagon. Later we had a couple of pickup trucks and would haul the grain in fifty-five-gallon drums. We could haul seven at a time. Here is where I learned the fine art of barrel rolling. I could move two hundred pounds with relative ease. Where we picked up the grain was scary. It looked like a place they could have filmed the *Children of The Corn* horror movie. Whenever we made this trip after a rain, getting stuck in the mud became a major issue. When I turned sixteen, then Mark a year later, we were the ones who usually picked up the grain for Dad. This wasn't our most beloved chore.

Baling Hay

To cut the hay crop, Dad used a sickle hay mower that mounted to the H tractor. It had razor-sharp triangular blades on a bar that quickly rotated back and forth to cut the hay. This was a really dangerous piece of equipment. Sometimes Dad would accidently hit a setting hen pheasant. If only her legs were cut, we might have her for supper. After the hay was cut, we waited usually two days for it to dry. Then with the rake we would windrow the hay. The rake was pulled to one side so the tractor would not drive over and damage the cut hay. Once the hay was raked, then we were ready to bale. The rake was also used to windrow straw so it could be baled. We were baling straw on Mr. Jones's farm, located on Highway 31 north of Highway KR. Kevin was pulling our rake down the lane and forgot the rake stuck a few feet out to the side. Before he realized what had happened, he had pulled out about a hundred yards of pasture fence.

Dad had a hayfield north of our house on the west side of the driveway, probably about five acres. He had another ten-acre hayfield along our north border, next to Highway KR. Once Dad was raking this five acres, preparing the field to bale. I was five or six years old when I decided to surprise Dad by hiding under a windrow of hay. When he spotted me about three rows from his tractor and rake he went ballistic. At the time I didn't appreciate the danger of the situation. That was probably one of the few times I was ever paddled.

The hay-loader was a tall machine that picked up windrows of loose hay. The hay went up over the top and dropped onto the following wagon down below. Using gravity, it was easier for the man on the wagon to move the hay and pile it. Once hay balers were invented, hay-loaders became obsolete quickly.

We owned two hay wagons. Whenever we needed more, we borrowed some from the neighbors. Our wagons were built on old truck chassis. A typical wagon measured eight by fourteen feet. One summer we built two wagon racks with heavy planks that came from Almando Ricchio's barn, which Dad had torn down.

Because our wagons sat outside all year, it was important to protect the wood from the weather. When we finished building the racks, we boys painted them with creosote, the same stuff used to preserve telephone poles, which last for decades. Creosote stinks and looks like used motor oil, and it burns when it touches your skin.

Wagons usually had a standard, a gate at the back, which helped hold the bales straight up and down. It was important not to put too much weight against the standard or it could break off when we hit a big hole with a wagon wheel. It was never fun when we had to reload a wagon from the ground.

If the wagon tires were good, we would put more than a hundred bales on a load. A big load was one hundred twenty bales. When Dad wasn't around we competed to see who could build the "monster" load. I think the record was one hundred forty-four bales nine layers high on a fourteen by eight-feet wagon. These big loads put quite a strain on the tires. We replaced a lot of wagon tires growing up. If the load wasn't solid, it came tumbling down, adding to our dilemma.

St. Catherine's High School used to borrow our wagons to build floats for the homecoming parade in the fall. On an occasion or two Dad even lined up a neighbor's wagon for a float. Dad was always very generous, helping anyone in need. Dad grew up in the Depression, and he knew most people worked hard for everything they owned. There was nothing that upset Dad more than a thief. I guess I would put people who steal and those who damage others' property in the same category. Needless to say, he wasn't happy when he learned that one of the floats was set on fire during the homecoming football game. Thankfully, Dad was reimbursed for the damage done to his wagon.

From 1910 until the late 1950s, hayforks were used to put loose hay and straw into the mows. Each wagon would be pulled into the barn for unloading. Four hayforks that looked like giant ice tongs were jabbed into the loose hay or straw. This pile then was lifted to the steel track that ran the length of the barn at the peak of the roof. The hay was sent flying to the designated mow and dropped in a heap. When square bales, which were actually rectangular in shape, were invented, farmers used the same hayforks to lift a seven-hundred-pound load of ten bales to the correct haymow. I barely remember Dad's crew moving both loose hay and bales using the hayforks. The invention of the hay baler and elevator quickly made hayforks obsolete. Bales were much easier to move than loose hay.

Farmers unloaded bales from wagons onto an elevator, which could be easily moved from mow to mow.

With each new invention, less labor was required. One hundred years ago, farmers were still using horses. Today's hay crop is probably produced with less than ten percent of what we needed years ago. Before automation, no farm chore was possible without tremendous physical strength. On our farm, making or baling hay was labor intensive. First, the hay was mowed and run through a crimper, which helped squeeze out the moisture. When dry, it was raked into windrows, then baled, and put onto wagons. From there hay went into the barn.

Most of our baling was done in the decade of the 1960s before big round balers were invented. Bales usually weighed sixty to seventy pounds and every bale was handled several times before it finally rested safely in the barn.

Our first baler was a twine bale Roanoke. We operated it with a gas engine. Sometimes the hay would be too thick and we had to stop the tractor and baler to prevent it from plugging. When it did plug, we had to shut everything off and pull the hay out of the machine by hand. Our problem was that neither of our tractors, the International H or the John Deere A, had a live power take-off. With live power, you can let the baler continue feeding the thick hay into the baler without it plugging. Sometimes after a plug, our baler would be out of time and the two needles would break as they pushed up through the bale chamber. Needles were cast iron and two feet long, expensive to replace, time-consuming to remove, and necessitated a run to the New Holland dealership for more.

Every time the plunger pushed hay into the bale chamber, the tractor, baler, and wagon all jerked for a moment then continued forward. Needles fed the twine up from the bottom through the bale. When the two ends of the twine met at the knotter, it was supposed to tie a knot. Mark and I, probably six and seven, would ride on top of the twine compartments on the right and left of the bale as it came through the machine. Each bale had two twine strings holding it together.

Our job was to tie a square knot every time the knotter didn't work, which was about every five or six bales. A square knot is always tied left over right then step two is right over left. If you did it backward, that was a granny knot that wouldn't stay tied. At that young age, our focus probably wasn't too great and we probably tied a lot of grannies. We spent hours riding the baler. For us it was a great job, we didn't have to work too hard, we were in the middle of the action, yet out of the way. Baling was loud and dusty, part of the reason for my hearing loss today. The best part was that every Friday night during hay season Dad would take all of his workers out for a fish fry.

One time a friend, Steve Gatske, fell trying to get a bale stuck in the chute onto the wagon. The front wheels of the wagon ran over his front legs. Fortunately, all the weight was on the back tires and he was unhurt. Can you imagine today having your children ride on a baler in front of a moving wagon weighing up to three tons. When we were ten and eleven, Mark and I started greasing this baler before baling each crop of hay. At that early age, Mark loved this chore, and I learned anything mechanical was not going to be in my future. This baler had about fifty grease fittings, all of which were impossible to get to, or so I thought. It was filthy work. I would have preferred a beating.

Our second baler was an Oliver, but these were tied with wire instead of twine. We had it for only one season. The bales were difficult to handle and Dad probably thought too dangerous for teenagers to operate. Once between balers we needed hay for our livestock, so Dad bought little round bales, probably fifty pounds apiece, from a farmer in Kenosha. These were hard to grab onto when you were trying to stack them. These never became too popular, because you always had to use a hay hook to move them. These, according to Dad, caused many wrist injuries.

Our third baler was a Case. Mark and I went with Dad to make the purchase. The woman's husband had died, and the baler had sat idle for several years. She was asking two hundred fifty dollars. Dad got it for one hundred twenty-five. We had it for many years. Both Mark and I operated it as well as Tim, my junior by six years. One time with this baler, Chucky Hartig, our neighbor, got too close and the power take-off shaft grabbed his shirt right off his back. It's a good thing he was a strong kid and could resist the pull. His strength saved his life.

One time, Dad sold two or three semi-loads of straw to a guy. I don't remember if this man wrote Dad a bad check, or if he said he had forgotten his checkbook. Dad made several calls and a trip or two to his home in Illinois to no avail. How could someone steal from a father struggling to support eleven kids? Even after that experience, Dad continued to trust every stranger who came to our door.

Custom Baling

In our family we all grew early. By eighth grade we were as tall as we were going to get. Growing early for the boys was a real advantage on the farm. We were taller, faster, and stronger than most of our friends. By age

58

ten we milked the cow and cleaned barns. At twelve we were baling hay and doing other chores that required the strength of a man. Dad always worked either at American Motors or construction jobs, so most of our baling was done by us boys. One summer we custom-baled and our oldest crewmember, Tom, was thirteen. Mike was twelve.

Besides baling for Dad, Mark and I started baling hay and straw for various neighbors by the time we were twelve. We especially liked working for Ray Lichter. He paid pretty well, and his cute daughter Renee always drove the baler in her bikini top. Even though she wouldn't give us the time of day, she sure was pleasing to look at.

Once we baled hay for our family's pediatrician, who owned a property over by Highway KR and Lathrop Avenue, not far from Lake Michigan. On summer nights the temperature in this area often dropped thirty degrees, and large deposits of dew were caused by the humidity from the lake. Even when the sun shone at this location, it took three days before hay was ready to bale.

This doctor agreed that he would have someone else move the hay to his horse barn just off of Highway 38, on the north side of Racine, when we were finished baling it. Once the baling was started, we learned that this irresponsible person had not arranged for the shipment of his eight hundred bales of prime hay. To prevent this hay from being damaged by rain, we agreed to haul it the ten miles to his beautiful farm. Our wagons were never built for hauling large loads long distances. Our wagons measured eight by fourteen feet and they each held one hundred bales. Using our ten-year-old grass green 1960 Ford pickup, we pulled all eight loads of hay to their destination using Highway 31. Thousands of people used this route daily on their way to and from work. It was the busiest road connecting Racine and Kenosha.

We encountered a lot of screaming, cursing motorists along the way. These ugly people weren't too happy with our hay wagons traveling at twenty-five miles per hour. We brought traffic almost to a standstill. At one point our friend Kevin, sixteen at the time, got so frustrated he leaned out the passenger window to his waist and stuck his two middle fingers in the face of one complaining driver on our right.

Because these wagons were not built for this wear and tear, we had five flat tires during this adventure. It was dangerous jacking up a wagon weighing seven thousand pounds, and then leaving it on the gravel shoulder while we took the wheel to have the tire fixed. There were no cell phones back then. The thanks we got for saving this customer's hay was he didn't pay us. After several months we were notified that we had an unpaid bill from the doctor's office. Mom informed the secretary that our bill was a fraction of what the doctor owed us. He eventually paid up.

The strongest workers were always in the haymow. Once we demonstrated we could do a man's work, we were always assigned to the mow, thus the term "mowing" hay, with "mow" rhyming with "cow." We carried the sixty- to seventy-pound bales and stacked them in layers all the way to the top of the barn. Sometimes we would have to throw bales several feet high while stacking them. For us kids, even though it was tough, dirty work, we took much pride in doing the work of a man.

My wife, Audrey, grew up on a dairy farm, so for her family baling hay went on for twenty years longer than it did for my brothers and me. Several times after I became an adult I helped with the baling. Each time I thought, How could this have been fun? Several people Mark and I knew from college explained that when they grew up and left, the milk cows were on the next truck out, also leaving the farm.

The hay elevator was a crucial farm tool for putting hay into the barn. Without an elevator, the work probably would have increased threefold. Dad had a New Idea elevator with an electric motor. One year, Dad had hay and straw in three different barns: Mr. Corbett's, Mr. Damen's, and ours. We would move the elevator to different spots when we were putting hay or straw in a barn. Whenever we wanted to raise the elevator, we had to use a hand crank. As the cable tightened, the elevator would lift higher into the air. With each full circle with the crank we probably raised the elevator a quarter inch. Several hundred cranks was hard work for young kids, so we took turns. It wouldn't have been so bad if we weren't raising and lowering the elevator every time we moved to a new haymow, which was numerous times each summer.

Every time we had to haul the elevator to a new location, or when we weren't using it, it had to be lowered so it wouldn't tip over. This was the fun part. We would whip the crank; the weight of the elevator along with the release of the tension would lower it. The crank would fly like the blades of a windmill in a storm. It was too dangerous to try to stop by hand. Trying to stop a spinning crank when lowering the elevator was even more hazardous than starting a vehicle with a crank before the invention of electric starters. When the elevator went down to the desired height, we held a two-by-four to the spinning crank to stop it with a jolt.

Most hay raised in our area was either alfalfa for the cows to eat or timothy and brome that was fed to horses. After hay was cut, it normally took a day or two before it was ready to be raked into windrows for baling. On occasion if it was sunny and hot, hay might be ready for baling in as little as one day. One farm we custom baled was on Highway KR about a mile from Lake Michigan. Here the dew is so heavy on the hay each night that it takes extended time to dry properly. This farm raised clover, which is coarse and requires even more drying time. Some years by the lake, if humidity was high, it could be four days before the hay was ready to bale. Hay baling season was really a stressful time for Dad. Once downed hay is rained on, it becomes worthless. The exception would be if the rain comes before the hay starts to dry. This farm wasn't typical; here the farmer stored empty coffins in the barn. Whenever we had any down time waiting for a hay wagon to return or were waiting for a ride to go home, we would play Hide and Seek in and among the caskets.

Years ago, farmers didn't cut their first-crop hay until the second or third week of June. They believed the hay was most nutritious when all of the blossoms were in full bloom. Most summers we would only get two crops of hay. The second cutting would be in August. Every third or fourth year we would get lucky and harvest a third crop if the rains and hot weather cooperated. The first crop was our biggest. It was coarser and often had weeds in it. We might get one hundred bales an acre. Second crop was much better quality, with only half the volume. Like the grass in your lawn, it is much thinner than in early summer. Because it rains less in July and August, we usually were able to harvest our second crop rain-free. When we did get a third crop, it produced half the amount of the second but was of even better quality. On those occasions Dad sold it to the Racine Zoo. They paid top dollar, probably three or four times what a buyer would pay for first crop.

If hay gets rained on while lying in the field, it loses almost all of its nutrient value. Some years, that was thirty percent of our first crop. Damaged hay was probably Dad's biggest frustration farming. Whenever it happened, we stacked the bad hay by the woods and the following spring used it for mulch on our raspberries. Dad used to always say when it was dry and we were desperate for rain, "I should just mow the hay and that is sure to bring the rains." Dad learned years later that it usually rained during the solstice, when we were trying to bale our first crop of hay. Today farmers cut and bale the hay much earlier and more often. They cut the first crop in May. The yield is smaller but the hay quality is better. Then the later cuttings are better quality with more volume. Today farmers sometimes get a fourth crop.

Mom always brought us lunches when we baled. I remember the most popular one was tuna salad, sweet corn, and potato chips. We sometimes would have a cooler for water. I also remember bringing wide-mouthed glass gallon jars filled with water. These would be set in the shade of tall grass at the end of the field.

Growing up we never ate out much with eleven kids, except when we went out for fish. Friday night fish fries were a big treat throughout the summer. In Wisconsin, fish fries are very popular. Many restaurants and bars have fish specials on Fridays. When we were kids, Dad would treat all of us to fish on Friday night as a reward if we had helped with the baling during the week. We loved these outings throughout our growing up.

Usually our option was fried fish or shrimp, baked potato or fries. Places I remember were The Center of The World, Ken and Babe's, and Smitty's, which we called Harmie's because that was the nickname of the owner of Smitty's. To this day fish is still my favorite meal out. In 2013 we visited Ireland and Northern Ireland, and in our eight days there, I ate fish and chips the first six.

I remember the night President Kennedy was assassinated. We went to a fish fry at St. Catherine's in Racine, but it was pretty somber; our family's hero had just been killed.

Jobs We Kids Worked

Coming from a big family, we all started working early. My older sisters Mary and Ellen both earned their spending money and college money working as waitresses at the Country Kitchen, the restaurant at the end of our property. They were both great workers, but very quiet. Jane was a waitress all through high school, too, but with her sanguine personality, she talked and joked with all the patrons, breaking all the tip records for this establishment.

Mike, Steve, and I worked as dishwashers on Sundays, the busiest day of the week. We went to 6:30 a.m. Mass, then worked a four-hour shift that concluded with a free meal. I always ate the turkey, dressing, and mashed potatoes.

Once I proved myself a diligent dishwasher, I was promoted to assistant cook. This was a job I really enjoyed. Because we boys at home always did the outside chores, I had never worked in a kitchen. It opened a whole new world to me.

On my first day the cook told me, "Mash the potatoes." I didn't know you were supposed to drain the water first. My boss, a great trouble-shooter, added instant potatoes. I hope the customers who came in for real potatoes never found out.

Annetta Ramcke, a wonderful old neighbor, was the owner. At her home, she cooked the main entrée and baked all the pastries and desserts that were served. The restaurant had only ten tables, each seating four, and a counter that served six to eight others.

On Sundays, there was always a long waiting line to get served. The food was delicious, the best anywhere around. The restaurant was small, because housed in the other end of the building were a small grocery store and living residence. I remember Grandma Mueller, who was seventy-seven when I was born, taking me, as a young child, to eat at Annetta's restaurant for my birthday on a couple of occasions.

Annetta retired and closed her restaurant when Jane was going away to college in 1977. Annetta and her sister-in-law, Ollie, gave Jane the car I talked about in my first book, *Come Drive With Me*. It was an old black Rambler sedan still smelling a little of sour milk from its days as a milk delivery vehicle when Annetta purchased milk from Mom.

Tom and Mike were golf caddies at Petrifying Springs County Park during high school, and they worked with a number of local farmers who grew potatoes, cabbages, and onions. They also worked planting onion sets, the small plants that get transplanted the following year to produce full size onions.

Mary, Ellen, and Jane babysat a lot growing up, along with Steve and Mike on occasion. They had a lot of practice at home as they helped Mom raise our family. Donna and Beth were much younger, and I was long gone by the time they reached middle school and became old enough to babysit. Donna babysat quite a bit. Beth worked at Thrifty Mac's while in high school.

Mark and I were in fifth grade when we worked the Christmas season for Campbell's Tree Farm north of Sturtevant. Mrs. Campbell was one of our teachers at St. Sebastian. I don't remember much about our duties, but I do remember it was freezing cold and we were pretty young.

When Mark and I were in sixth grade we worked Saturdays helping Grandpa Wirtz. At the time he was in his seventies and difficult, a retired genius who had designed tractor parts for J.I. Case Company. One of Dad's close friends, Buster Gagnon, a jack-of-all-trades himself, used to work with Mr. Wirtz. He said it was no picnic.

Mr. Wirtz owned land on the edge of Sturtevant. When he decided to subdivide his property, he hired my brother Mike and some of his high school buddies to help tear down his old barn.

Mr. Wirtz was slow and methodical. He wasn't too happy with some of Mike's impatient friends when they started knocking down walls with a sledgehammer before he was ready. It was our job to help clean up the place.

We started at fifty cents an hour. Mr. Wirtz liked our work, so we got a raise to sixty cents. Included with our pay was a one-hour lunch break when his wife, our school cook, served us a feast each Saturday.

Grandpa Wirtz was a devout man. Early in their marriage, Mrs. Wirtz had become deathly ill. Grandpa Wirtz promised God if she were healed, he would give one week each year in service to St. Sebastian Church. For the rest of his life, he worked on church repairs and projects.

Our neighbor Ray Lichter had a small milk herd. Dad used to buy Ray's Holstein bull calves and Angus-Holstein cross calves. I remember Dad paying ten dollars for a day-old calf. About the time we reached high school, Ray took a forty-hour-a-week job and needed some extra help at home. Mark worked for him on Saturdays and for a couple of summers. Ray's wife, Snooky, was a great cook.

Once Mark got to college, he left the Ray Lichter farm and went to work farming for Al and Norm Wilks. Mom said Ray wasn't too happy when Mark left his employ. Who could blame Mark, it was for better pay and more hours, which paid for his college education.

When we were growing up, there were four mink farms within a mile-and-a-half of our home. Except for the Bydaleks, they all went out of business after Canadian competition made fur farming unprofitable for Wisconsinites. The Bydalek mink farm lasted for years because they diversified into animal byproducts. The summer after our freshman year of high school, Mark and I worked there boxing cattle byproducts for the manufacture of canned dog food. Ninety percent of other new hires lasted about an hour, but Mark and I stuck it out. After cattle were butchered at the Milwaukee stockyard, the cattle byproducts were shipped to Bydaleks in fifty-five-gallon barrels. Mark and I emptied the barrels and organized the byproducts into boxes to be frozen for shipment. We also cleaned cow tripe. All of the grass had to be rinsed out before the stomach could be frozen. In the tripe we sometimes found chunks of metal. To prevent hardware disease, some farmers fed to each calf a finger-sized magnet that would stay in the cow's stomach for life. The magnet collected any nails or metal that the cow accidentally swallowed, preventing the cow's stomachs from puncturing. For me, the two worst boxing tasks were rinsing slunk calves from pregnant cows that had been butchered, and cleaning cow udders that smelled like rotten milk. What we boxed was frozen, then shipped to dog food factories. There the byproducts were ground up and made into canned dog food. Don't ever eat dog food. Once

I recovered from the initial shock of this working environment, my biggest complaint was never being able to get the smell off my hands. That August, I quit working at Bydaleks to play sophomore football. Mark stayed and worked there for another year. Kevin Young, the friend we grew up with, became their box maker and stayed a couple of years.

I worked at A&W Drive-In the summer I was seventeen. It was a great job. We worked hard, but had a great boss and crew, and our customers loved coming to the drive-in. When my older brother Tom was drafted into the service, he left his old Dodge for us to drive. This car shifted with push buttons that were mounted on the dash. The reverse didn't work, so every day I had to park it facing forward so I could get out at the end of my shift, usually at 11 p.m. or midnight. A&W is famous for its root beer served in cold glass mugs and for its carhops. Even though ours didn't wear roller skates, most made pretty good tips. Any time a mug handle had a chip in the handle, we were allowed to bring it home. Customers considered these mugs a prize, so they disappeared frequently and always needed replacing. When a batch of root beer got old, it fermented and had to be thrown away. You couldn't have customers getting drunk at the local drive-in.

Other main A&W offerings were burgers, onion rings, fries, malts, and shakes. We served a Baby Burger of a single patty, a Momma Burger of two patties, and a Papa Burger of three patties. It was the first time I had ever tasted onion rings, and I have loved them ever since. Malts were pretty popular. If a customer preferred a plain milkshake, we just didn't add the squirt of malt mix. Hamburgers were made with a secret seasoning. An orange powder and a little water were mixed with a tub of hamburger, drained, and then made into dozens of round balls. These were then smashed on the grill for cooking. The floors used to get slippery with grease from the fryers and open grills. Cleaning the restaurant at closing each night was an important part of our job, especially mopping the floor. We also emptied and cleaned the shake machines, scrubbed the grills, and replaced grease in the fryers when needed. I brought two milk cans to put behind the restaurant. My boss let me bring home the milk from the shake machines. Dad had some pigs in a pen at the southeast end of our woods. With the sour milk, they ate well all summer. Eventually the pigs did have to be brought back to the barn, because neighbor dogs were attacking and injuring them. I was paid $1.40 an hour, which was five cents over minimum wage in 1970. It was a great job. I planned to work there the following summer and get Mark a job also. As it turned out, I didn't apply early enough that spring, and neither of us was employed there in 1971.

During our Thanksgiving break senior year, Mark and I got to work loading a ship in Kenosha on Lake Michigan. I believe it was a relief shipment they were anxious to get out of the harbor before the winter freeze. It was fascinating. I had never been on a ship. Each shift was four hours long. It was like hiring day laborers today. A crowd of men willing to work gathered at the ship. Each foreman would count off the number he needed, and anyone not selected would go home. By hand we loaded forty-pound sacks of flour and sixty-eight-pound blocks of butter. It wasn't too much different from stacking hay in the mow. Even with a couple of wrestling practices over that four-day break, I worked several four-hour shifts.

I was eighteen, and Mark seventeen. He was able to work a couple of shifts before they discovered he wasn't yet eighteen, the legal age to do this work. Uncle Hank had an old AMC car he gave us. The engine was going bad and left a smoke trail for blocks. When driving it, you had to be careful not to accelerate too quickly, or people would think you were on fire. The car wasn't very sound environmentally, but it did get me to and from Lake Michigan to the ship, which gave me Christmas spending money that season.

Mark was supposed to start working after the first of the year at a Sturtevant gas station. I took his job after the wrestling accident that injured his neck. When he recovered in the spring, we both worked at the station. That was back when you still pumped a customer's gas and cleaned the windshields. Back then, the gas cap was found in some unusual places.

Our 1956 Chevy's gas cap was hidden behind the back left tail light in the fender. The guy who managed the station was either an idiot or was a crook. It didn't matter how careful we were balancing our accounts at the end of each shift, he would dock everyone's wages every pay period for supposed mistakes we had made.

Wisconsin's drinking age turned eighteen on a Wednesday night in March of 1972. I was a senior in high school, and almost nineteen. Tom and Mike were back from the service, so I met them at midnight to celebrate at a bar called C.C.R. It was one of their hangouts at High Street and Main.

Tom, Mike, and I all worked summer construction jobs. I used my income from construction work to get my college education. Because work was plentiful in the mid-1960s, Mike even got a special permit to work at age seventeen. One Friday a jackhammer smashed his toe, but he was back on the job Monday morning.

66

After working many years in construction, Dad gave me this advice: "Never stop moving. If there isn't anything else to do, pick up a broom and sweep." This counsel I used putting myself through college, and during the past forty-two years in education. During these years, I have been blessed to work with more than seven thousand students.

Though I was a hard worker, I was always trying to figure out a better, more efficient way to do every job, and I hated anything mechanical. By age ten I knew I was not going to make a living with my hands. When working with Dad, I thought he looked for the most difficult way to complete a task, and that was how we always did it. I think he thought I was just lazy. We never got along too well until I was an adult and no longer had to work with him. After I graduated from high school, he was pleasantly surprised when numerous construction friends reported back that I was a great worker. I do remember coming home from work sometimes and falling asleep on the living room floor.

The union hall found me only three jobs in my five years of working construction. The first was in 1971, when I was eighteen years old between my junior and senior year. I was called to a job site where they had two-and-a-half days of work.

The second job they found me was the next summer. I worked on the new water treatment plant being built along Lake Michigan in Oak Creek, north of Racine. In 1973 I used my contacts from the previous summer to gain employment at the same job site, but with a different contractor. That year I got my older brother Tom a job on our crew. During our lunch breaks we would play three-handed Sheepshead. Both years we worked on twenty parallel concrete water treatment tanks, each holding a million-and-a-half gallons of water.

In 1974, I once again found work using my contacts from the two previous summers. That was a blessing, because construction jobs were scarce during the early 1970s. This time I worked road construction, mainly putting in intersections. The concrete poured at intersections was required to be at least seven inches thick. Construction workers had a special name for my boss's intersections because cement was never seven inches throughout, only along the edges. Back then they used to joke that job superintendents' Christmas bonuses were based on how much concrete they cheated the state out of.

In 1975, Dad was working a big sewer construction job in Racine. On this job were four or five highly trained workers from inner-city Milwaukee, who were specialists in this type of construction. One Friday night these construction workers found themselves stranded. Their car wouldn't start, and they had no connections in Racine. Dad intervened and called his best friend, Sammy, who lived nearby. Sammy was a mechanic and had them on their way in no time. These construction workers were really appreciative of Dad's help. They didn't realize that Dad spent his whole life living the Golden Rule.

Dad decided to leave the sewer construction job and go back to work at American Motors that spring when my classes at Loras were finished for the summer. Because of Dad's reputation, and his recommendation, I took over his position at the sewer construction job. That summer, averaging eleven hours a day, I got a lot of overtime. That was a good thing because I was saving for my last year of college. I bought my first car, a robin's egg blue 1972 Gremlin, and Audrey and I bought her engagement ring and our wedding bands.

There was a cave-in on the job that spring, fifty feet below ground. Fortunately, no one died. A co-worker did break his arm in two places that day, but he was back to work four weeks later. Two weeks after that, on my twenty-second birthday, he was operating an air spade, a machine weighing seventy pounds that was used to dig the clay for the new tunnel we were creating.

My job was to pull all the clay chunks away from where he was piling them. It was physically the hardest day I had ever worked. His job was worse than mine, but at the end of the day he just stretched his arm a couple of times and his comment was, "That arm is kind of sore."

Audrey came into Kenosha, and we took Mom and Dad out to eat. I think they were expecting some good news, but I was so tired I fell asleep while we ate. They were disappointed that night, but on July 4 we announced our engagement. Mom and Dad were thrilled that I was going to marry such a sweet farmer's daughter. Later, Mom and Dad also thought it was funny that whenever Audrey came to visit, she didn't know how to pick anything. She grew up on a dairy farm, not a truck farm.

I graduated from Loras College a year later on May 8, 1976. Audrey and I were married Memorial Day weekend, on May 29. I was hired to start teaching in the fall at Saint Anthony's Grade School in Dubuque, Iowa. That summer we came back to Racine to work. Audrey and I lived with my oldest brother, Tom, then a bachelor, in Rubberville.

Audrey worked as a cashier at one of Benson Oil's gas stations in Racine, in a neighborhood that wasn't very nice. My younger brother Steve worked there also that summer. Their boss shared with them that this particular store was the only station they owned without bulletproof glass.

I worked a few weeks for Kremis Farms repairing buildings and picking rocks and helped Al and Norm Wilks build grain bins. The rest of the summer I worked bridge construction, sometimes fifty feet in the air.

After Dad injured his back in 1966, Al and Norm Wilks, two brothers in their twenties, started renting our farm in 1968. Norm recently died. Fifty years later, the Wilks Brothers still rent our farm, along with six thousand other acres. Al's son Don, now in his mid-fifties, works with his Dad in the family business. Don said, "I might retire before Dad."

Mark started working for the Wilks Brothers Farms after his first year of college. It was a great fit, considering Mark was an agriculture major at University of Wisconsin-Platteville. He worked summers, school breaks, and Saturdays when he came home on weekends. I remember being invited to at least one New Year's Eve shop party that was a lot of fun for anyone who enjoyed beer. After graduation, Mark worked for a big farmer in Walnut, Illinois. He and Barbara, newly married and far from family and friends, decided after one year to move back home. Mark went back to work for Al and Norm Wilks for their ever-expanding business for ten enjoyable years, until another opportunity became available. The Wilks family members are still close family friends to this day.

Steve worked at McDonald's during high school from July 1974 until August 1975. If Steve had known what McDonald's was going to become, maybe today he would be a rich retired franchisee.

Thrifty Mac's was a one-of-a-kind hardware store on Lathrop Avenue in Racine. It was a handyman's paradise. They had merchandise other stores hadn't seen in decades. Because merchandise cost a little more, some people hesitated to shop there. If it was hard to find in Racine or Kenosha, Thrifty Mac's was where they finally ended up. Thrifty Mac's owners taught their hardworking employees how to advise do-it-yourself customers on how to complete their projects. Our neighbor Chuck worked at Thrifty Mac's, and his recommendation helped Tim get a job there. This is where Tim became a jack-of-many-trades. He worked at the store through high school and on summer breaks when he was in college. Tim's boss loved his attitude and work ethic and wanted him to pursue his future in the hardware business. Tim decided to chase a college degree instead. Maybe having eight older siblings who all went to college had some impact on his career plan.

Beth also worked at Thrifty Mac's as a teenager and young adult. She never became a projects expert like her brother. She was content to pay her way through college as a summertime cashier.

Dad gets ready for the day near the east side of our barn, where Mark and I built our pigeon coop. Above, the pigeon coop was built on one of the sides of the barn that got painted.

Chapter 4: This Old Barn, Our Playground

For Mark and me, the barn was not only our main workstation, it was our playground that we enjoyed until we left home. Mark and I built our forts and tunnels, and we played exciting and dangerous games of roundup and hide-and-seek. This is where we had many of our sleepovers, and where Mark and I hosted our boy-girl parties and barn dances following in the footsteps of Mike and Tom.

The original barn owned by Grandpa Peter Mueller and his brother Mike burned down and was rebuilt around 1910. Dad wasn't born until eight years later when his father, Peter, was almost fifty years old.

Our barn was thirty-seven feet by eighty feet and thirty-five feet tall. The building ran north to south. The middle space, called the barn floor, rose all the way to the barn roof. To the north were two haymows above the horse barn. To the south, were three haymows above the cow barn. Because the barn floor was in the center of the barn, it saw the most traffic. It had big doors on both the east and west walls so two wagons full of hay could be pulled in when needed. They were parked inside if rain was forecast, or if the hay was for sale and wasn't going to be mowed.

On the south side of the barn floor was a concrete feed tank where we stored all of our ground feed. The tank walls were six inches thick. It stood three feet wide, seven feet long, and three-and-a-half feet tall. It was built many years before Grandpa's death in 1946. He wrote his name, *Peter Mueller,* on the tank wall while the cement was still wet. When the barn blew down in the early 1990s, my brothers cut out Grandpa's concrete signature from the feed tank. Today it still sits on Mom and Dad's front porch.

Because we didn't have a lot of cattle or hogs, we used an antique hammer mill from the early 1900s to grind all our own feed. Today farmers use grinders to chop and mix their livestock feed. Some do it themselves, others have it custom done. All of our livestock were fed ground feed. This was a mixture of corn and oats, or when we had it, barley and oats. These were dumped into the hammer mill and ground. The mill sat right next to the concrete feed tank, and was screwed into the cement floor. Grinding was dusty, dirty work. Fortunately, a batch of ground feed would last for weeks. The mill weighed hundreds of pounds and was too heavy to lift. Sometimes the mill had to be moved so we could get wagons of hay out of the weather and under roof. We used to roll the mill on steel poles west of the feed tank and out of the way.

When Mike was a freshman, his class built a float in our barn floor using one of our hay wagons. They made three giant soapboxes. Their slogan for the float was, "Let's CHEER them on, to turn the TIDE, and DASH to victory." These boxes next to each other ran fourteen feet, the length of the wagon. They were eight feet tall and two feet wide. The plan was for Mark Poplawski, inside, to launch balloons out the top of the boxes to look like bubbles. When the wagon pulled onto the highway, however, the breeze created by the float in movement sent bubbles flying all the way to town.

The south end of the barn was the cow barn, which occupied fifty percent of the first floor. Dad milked twenty cows here, ten cows on each side, their heads facing the center with a walkway in between for easier feeding. Our silo was connected to the barn on the far south end. It was designed so silage could be thrown down from above and then wheeled right in to feed the cows.

In the early 1950s, the state did some roadwork on Highway 31. They needed fill dirt for the project, so Dad sold them the hill that was behind the barn. When the excavating crew was moving earth, they must have hit the field tile for the silo drain. A few years later, in 1956, when Dad sold his milk herd and the silo was emptied of silage, he noticed water in the bottom of the silo that indicated the silo drain did not work properly. When we were growing up, the silo sat with several feet of water and sludge in it for years. This pit was dangerous, and we had strict orders never to play in the silo. That may be the only instruction we ever really obeyed.

The north end of the barn was smaller and we called this the horse barn, because when Dad was growing up this is where Grandpa Peter Mueller kept the Percheron draft horses, then later the bigger Belgians. This north section of our barn contained about one-third the space on the ground level. The only livestock I remember housed in that area were a few rabbits we raised for a time and chickens that would roost in the rafters. Dad's tractors, corn planter, and lumber occupied most of the space. Dad brought home discarded lumber from the many construction sites he had worked. He recycled most of the lumber that was being thrown away. The north wall of the horse barn had a garage door behind which Dad stored his Farmall H.

The barn was originally built to hold loose hay, which was not as heavy or compacted as baled hay. After Dad started putting baled hay into the mow in the late 1950s, some of the beams had to be shored up so the floor above could hold the added weight. He jacked up the standing posts and poured a concrete pad, raising them a few inches so the beams above wouldn't sag. Dad used to put three thousand bales of hay and straw into the barn. Mows one and two to the south of the barn floor had first-crop hay that was fed to the cattle. The third mow on the far south was where we stored our baled straw that was used for bedding. We sprinkled straw under the cows to keep them clean, dry, and more comfortable when lying on the concrete. Between the second and third mow, we had a chute for throwing down hay and straw bales so they landed right in front of the cows below. A close friend of my brother Mike's, Syl, fell to the cow barn floor when he didn't make it all the way across the hay chute above. Fortunately, he fell with a few bales of hay for cushion and was unhurt.

We sold hay for fifty cents a bale and straw for twenty-five cents a bale. Dad got twenty dollars a ton for hay. There were two mows to the north side of the barn that usually held second-crop hay. It was heavy and better quality hay. It brought a better price and was what Dad usually sold. When we did get a third crop of hay, Dad was able to sell that to the Racine Zoo for probably three times the price of first-crop hay.

The distance from the barn to the house was thirty yards. On dark winter nights, it sure seemed a lot farther for this little boy. Anytime I had to return to the house alone after nightfall, I always waited until there were no passing cars, then I ran as fast as I could. I never wanted anyone driving by on busy Highway 31 to see me walking to the house. I believed if I were seen, passers-by would think we had someone prowling in our yard. Youthful logic; to prevent intruders was the reason we always had a Collie watchdog. Was this considered being afraid of the dark? I'm guilty. My sister Mary once said she wasn't really afraid of the dark, just what might be lurking in it.

Much of the hay Dad sold was kept in the north mow. Sometimes by the time winter arrived, it would be empty. This is where we boys on occasion held our barn parties or dances. Dad and Larry Rashleger built a temporary staircase from the barn floor up to the north haymow, attached to the wall. When we needed to put wagons in the barn, this staircase was in the way. So eventually they cut a hole in the mow floor and connected the staircase from underneath. This proved to be both practical and convenient. When the mow was empty, we used to shoot buckets on a hoop we nailed to the north wall. Then we decided we wanted to do layups, so we mounted the basket one beam to the south. Though we goofed around up there, most of us became wrestlers, not basketball players. For a short time we even had an old pool table up there.

Mark and I used to invite friends overnight and then sleep in tents or, more often, in the haymow. By laying our sleeping bags on top of the hay or straw, we usually had a pretty comfortable bed where we were nice and cozy. With no curfew, some of those nights became pretty long. In 1967, when Mark and I were in eighth grade, we got a tape recorder for Christmas. Cassettes were brand new. One morning after sleeping in the mow we recorded our friend Mike Chiappe complaining, "I couldn't sleep because the f_ _ _ _ _ _ rooster was crowing all night." Then we kept repeating three seconds of it over and over. We thought it was much funnier than Mike did.

I lost much of my fear of heights at a young age while learning to climb the beams in the barn. They were fifteen feet above the concrete below. At the time it seemed more like fifteen yards. Roundup was our favorite game in the barn. It was a variation of tag and hide-and-seek. One person started out as It. As each player got tagged, he became part of the team that together had to find and tag all the remaining players before the round was over. You got good at playing roundup only if you could run across high beams and learn to take risks. Sometimes we had a tall ladder leaning up against the barn next to a big hole in the wall through which we put hay using the elevator. I remember being on the top of the ladder with one player above in the haymow and one climbing up from below. I waited until the person below got high enough up the steps, so he was afraid to jump. Then from above I hurtled over him to the ground and made my escape. It was also helpful if you were willing to jump eight feet to the concrete from the mow above. We also had some great hiding places in the haymow. Sometimes our hiding places were too good. After sitting quietly for a long time, we discovered that everyone else in frustration had quit the game a half hour earlier.

Stepping on a nail was always a danger when we played in the barn. When Mom and Dad were young, one of the Finks to the north died of lockjaw, a disease that resulted from tetanus in an infected wound. With eleven kids, it seemed that someone was always being taken to the doctor's office or the emergency room. Whenever we had a cut that required stitches or we stepped on a nail, we usually had to get a tetanus shot again to prevent lockjaw, because no one could ever remember the date of the last tetanus shot. I remember my skin being punctured on three occasions, although I'm sure there were more. Once I stepped on a board and nailed it flat to the bottom of my foot. That nail went pretty deep. I still have a scar on my foot from that one. Another time, Mike was fighting me using no hands. He pushed me onto the top of a toy sewing machine, embedding its one-inch top spindle into my butt. The third was one Friday afternoon when I ran my foot into a manure fork that was lying on a bale. I was in a hurry to leave for camping overnight at Kevin's, so I told no one until the next morning when my shoe wouldn't fit on my swollen foot. I got a pair of shots at the emergency room, two more on Monday, and the last two scheduled for Wednesday. We didn't go back because at my softball game the night before I was pretty mobile, and Mom decided we didn't need the added expense.

Mom believed for us to grow and learn, we had to experience all that farm life had to offer. It didn't always turn out as planned. My older siblings were once sliding down a board from one haymow to the next. What looked like a fun game had each child crying. After two or three bleeding bottoms, it was discovered that a protruding nail was causing the damage.

All livestock farms had rats and mice that were attracted by the grain that was fed to animals. We spent a lot of time playing in the mows in winter, and I don't ever remember seeing mice in the hay, though. One of my sisters claimed that she and friends were once sleeping in the barn and they had a mouse run over the top of their sleeping bag.

On most farms, cats called mousers killed and ate these unwanted intruders. Along with cats, farmers used rat poison. Cats alone weren't going to totally solve your rodent problems regardless of how well they hunted. I was told that it was important to give your cats fresh cow's milk daily to protect them whenever they ate a rat already killed by poison. I'm not sure if this is true.

Rats live near the source of their food. The best places on our farm to find rats were under the platform bed where the pigs slept in their pigpen, the corncrib, and the temporary sweet corn silo we constructed many summers. When we were hunting rats, our pigpen was the most dependable place to look. It was vital to remove all the manure from the pigpen before looking for rats under the platform. If you didn't, you were always in danger of splashing the manure or worse, slipping and falling in it.

Before combines were invented, farmers used to harvest their grain using threshing machines, which disturbed rats in the field. Old farmers we knew shared stories of panicked rats running right up a farmer's pant leg trying to escape. Using twine, some farmers would tie the bottom of their pants or put their pant legs inside their boots. Hunting rats was both exciting and scary. Mindful of these old farmers' tales, we always wore rubber boots in the pigpen both as a rodent deterrent and also to keep our shoes clean from the manure. You never knew how many rats were going to scurry when you moved the pig platform. The goal was to kill as many rats as possible using our shovels, manure forks, and cats. Our best weapon was a few good mousers. Next was the shovel, which was used to smash escaping rats. Over the years we broke a few shovel handles, which really ticked off Dad. Forks were our last choice. Silage forks were too wide and heavy to move quickly; pitchforks with only three prongs seldom hit their target. If you had to use a fork, the manure fork with four or five tines worked best. Forks of any kind were dangerous because they could inflict severe damage to a person's lower extremities. If it had been a while since a rat hunter had received a tetanus shot, being stabbed in the foot with a contaminated fork necessitated a trip to the doctor for the necessary shot.

Whenever we emptied the corncrib the rats would scurry. Each spring when we finished off the last of the sweet-corn silage, we could expect quite a few energized rats as well.

Mom used to shoo us boys from the house whenever possible. This gave us a lot of time during Christmas break and on snow days for building forts in the barn. Once Mark and I learned how to use a pulley, rope, and hay hooks, we became master builders. Then we could dig our forts all the way to the bottom of the haymow. Using lumber to cover our tunnels, we connected all of our forts. One year we had six forts: Three were on the south end of the barn, and three on the north, all joined by passageways. Each winter it was important for Dad to know how many bales of hay and straw he had in the barn. He needed enough feed for his livestock to make it until spring. Anytime Dad had extra, he would sell bales of hay and straw to help pay the bills during the lean, cold months. Whenever Dad discovered our forts, caverns where hay should have been, he would get really upset.

In the fall of 1966, when Mike was a senior, he hosted a barn dance for St. Catherine's students. Back then when a teenager's wages were barely more than a dollar an hour, Mike spent big bucks to hire a band for twenty dollars. At the football game, one of Mike's friends announced on the public address system that everybody was invited to the barn dance at the Mueller farm. Every kid in Racine knew about it, and hundreds showed up. The band played in the north haymow. Cars were parked in the orchard all the way down to the Country Kitchen Restaurant. Dad rounded up some of the fathers and together they became the security for this shindig. They spent the night parking cars, confiscating beer, and rousting young lovers from back seats. Not surprisingly, it became the social event of the year. Decades later, it was still referred to as the famous barn dance.

Three years later, Mike was drafted in August 1969. My brother Tom and Mike's friends decided to throw him a surprise going-away party the night before his departure. After a few beers, Mike's friends decided to shave Mike's head but leave his big red beard untouched. Fortunately, Mike was smart enough to remove his whiskers before departing for boot camp, although a couple of days later his sergeants didn't think his bald head was that funny.

At Mike's party, his friend Tad was arrested and served thirty days in jail under the Huber Law, which allowed him to work during the day and report to jail at night. Upon Tad's release, Tom threw Tad a party in our barn. It was another disaster. Between the north and south haymows was a log suspended fifteen feet above the concrete floor. It had been used years earlier a couple of times to butcher cows. After Tad got drunk, he thought he was Spider-Man. Tad fell attempting to walk the fourteen-foot unsecured log from one end to the other. The party ended abruptly, and Tad was transported by ambulance to the hospital with a cracked skull. Fortunately, he had no permanent injuries.

Mark and I had a boy-girl party in the barn when we were in eighth grade. We made cool barn-shaped invitations from red card stock. We copied the ones Mike had used years earlier for one of his parties. Our whole class was invited. I'm sure we had at least thirty kids, because Mom would never allow us to exclude anyone. Our party was held in the horse barn. There hadn't been horses in it for many years, but it was called that because when Dad was growing up that barn was the home of my Grandfather Peter's eight draft horses. We cleaned out all the stalls and had a pretty cool party. It would have been even better if it hadn't been so well chaperoned. When Mark and I were seniors in 1971, we hosted a barn dance, too. Once again, the barn was packed. The band decided it was too much work to haul all their equipment upstairs, so they played on the barn floor. Dancers went wild in both the north haymow and the horse barn below. By this time, bands were unionized and live music cost us more than two hundred bucks. Through the years, Dad often wondered how the haymow ever survived the weight of hundreds of bouncing teenagers.

Racing pigeons was another adventure Mark and I decided to try. Our friend Tony Rossi, at sixteen, was already the best pigeon racer in both Racine and Kenosha counties. Tony bought good birds and knew how to combine successful bloodlines when breeding. Racing pigeons have a lot of muscle, and they probably weigh three times as much as a wild pigeon. Tony had a training program for his pigeons similar to that of a successful track coach. Each day, Tony varied the birds' flight workout times, depending on how many days were left before the race and its distance. Races ranged in length from fifty to one thousand miles. Adult bird flying season was in the spring and early summer. Young bird season was in late summer and fall for the birds born in the spring. People refer to pigeon racing as the poor man's horse racing. Even back then, many racers had thousands of dollars invested in this hobby. Tony is the only one I know of who operated in the black.

Pictures of the front of our old barn after 1970 show a huge cage about ten feet off the ground with three windows going into the barn. This cage connected with the eight-foot by twelve-foot coop Mark and I built on the northeast corner of the haymow. It was divided into two sections. The bigger area to the north was for the older birds and included nesting boxes. The young birds were on the south end.

Our venture lasted two years until Mark and I went away to college. We didn't have the funds for this expensive hobby, and we weren't home to give our birds the proper care. We paid my younger brother to feed them while we were away. When the birds didn't get fed on schedule, they were pretty aggressive when anyone entered their coop. They weren't trying to harm anyone, they were just hungry. They acted like the pigeons seen in the movie *Home Alone*. This is when my six-year-old sister Beth developed her lifelong fear of birds. To this day, I am still fascinated by pigeon racing and the feats these birds can accomplish.

Across the driveway from the barn stood the pump house, or milk house. It is probably twelve feet square. Below the floor in the center of the room is the well. In the southwest corner there used to be a water tank that was used to cool the fresh milk after milking when Grandpa Peter and Dad milked. Dad quit milking a herd in 1956, so we began referring to the milk house as the pump house. Various tools were stored there. In the fall, the pump house was the storage place for apples that needed to be sold or eaten before the winter freeze.

Mom's hand-painted sign announces firewood for sale. This picture does not show the silo, which was taken down before it fell down. A shear wind later blew the barn down. In the background are Dad's apple trees.

Mark's business, Mueller Tree Service, harvests logs like these to saw into lumber for woodworkers and crafters. Selling firewood is also part of his business. For many years, Dad served as Mark's salesman.

Mom loved to catch up with all the news, and she kept the relatives informed on the latest happenings. Middle, family members enjoy an Easter dinner: Shawn, Vernay, Sunny, Mike, Bonny, Tom, Mary, Sally, Tim, Mom, Barbara, Mark. Bottom, a pleasant summer view of the east side of the house from the driveway.

Chapter 5: If This Old House Could Talk

Our house was the nerve center of the farm. Some of life's most important lessons were taught there, such as love, storytelling, card playing and fun. It is where our older brothers Mike and Tom rolled dice to take Mark's and my Easter candy. All decisions, appointments, schedules, and duties were organized and dispatched from the kitchen.

Our farmhouse was two different houses moved to one location. There is a basement under the whole house except under the old kitchen. The older part, built in 1850, makes the house almost one hundred seventy years old. After Grandpa Peter Mueller bought the farm about 1900, twenty-two children were raised in this old house, which still has only one bathroom. According to Dad, Grandpa's family had an indoor bathroom before most of their neighbors because a relative hated venturing out to the outhouse. Grandma Mary had a cousin with money from Chicago, who sometimes came to visit. He made the mistake of visiting the farm one frigid winter. During the night Nature called, requiring him to journey through sub-zero temperatures and snow to the outhouse. When he returned to Chicago, he sent money to the farm to have an indoor privy installed. Grandpa Peter went to Illinois and purchased a used sink, toilet, and tub. After the bathroom was installed, this relative never again had to make that bone-chilling trip out back to a frigid privy.

We didn't have a lot of rules, but the ones we had were dead serious. Never swear or you get your mouth washed out with soap. Never fight. Never scream when you're around the barn or farm equipment. Never play around running equipment. If you can't say anything nice, don't say anything at all. Always finish the job you start. Always pound down your nails. Never tie anyone up. Never cover the windows with blackout blankets when playing hide and seek. Never play in the creek. Once we boys turned eighteen, if you had too much to drink, never drive home, stay where you are. I know Mom was a lot more protective of the girls.

Mom and Dad seldom spanked us. Dad was always working, and Mom was the disciplinarian. When we misbehaved, she sent us upstairs, which was pure torture. There were no electronics back then, with absolutely nothing to do in our bedrooms. The black-and-white television and all games were in the playroom downstairs. Any time we were banished, we just hoped Mom's "mad" didn't last too long, or that she didn't forget we were up there. After a while we would draft someone to see how upset Mom really was. That person would sneak downstairs. If Mom yelled, "Stay up there," we knew our time-out wasn't yet over. If she didn't holler, we could all come back down.

When I was young, our address was Rural Route 4 Box 448. We had a Racine phone number, even though we lived on the Kenosha side of Highway KR that ran along the Kenosha-Racine county line. When we were little, we had a party line that I don't remember much about, except later our phone number was 414-633-2149. Mom talked a lot on the phone. She kept everyone informed of all family events — births, deaths, and everything in between. I know Dad used to get irritated with how much time Mom spent on the phone, but for decades she was the axle of both Dad's and her family wheels, keeping everything spinning. Mom remembered every person she ever met. She knew all eighty of their nieces and nephews, as well as how many children each had and where most were located at any given time. I wish I could remember how she did it, but Mom had a system for reaching family in Kenosha without having to pay the toll.

The phone system got changed when University of Wisconsin-Parkside was built in the 1960s. I guess officials decided that any call made by someone near the University should be a local phone call for parts of both Racine and Kenosha. Our new phone number then started with a 552. It was great for us, because now Mom could call her sisters in Kenosha without having to pay long distance fees.

Before the phone number change, I remember discussions at home when my brother Tom called up his girlfriend. She lived only a couple of miles away, but he was racking up huge long-distance charges. Then six years later, after Parkside was built, it was a local call when I talked to my girlfriend, a neighbor of Tom's former girlfriend. To this day, the phone still hangs on the wall between the kitchen and living room. When we were young, there was a little open recess next to the playroom door where we hung up our coats. I remember trying to hide in there as a middle schooler whenever I called a girl I was interested in. It was important my siblings not hear these conversations.

The main entry to our family's house was through a door on the wrap-around porch on the south and southeast sides. The front room was Mom and Dad's bedroom. With no privacy, it is amazing they ever had eleven kids. I do remember when we were little we would pile into bed with them on Saturday or Sunday mornings. The location of their bedroom didn't get changed until we were all grown. To the left of Mom and Dad's bedroom was the old kitchen on the south side of our house. From 1948 until 1957, Grandma occupied the two rooms to the north. When she moved to her trailer, the kitchen was moved to her old quarters in the north of the house because it was warmed by heat registers from the furnace. The old kitchen had been heated by wood, and didn't have any ductwork for heat. For the next sixty years, it became a huge storeroom. To the right of Mom and Dad's bedroom was the living room. Our playroom was to the northwest. The old shanty was west of the playroom. It had the only entrance to the basement where we kept our work clothes, boots, and the washing machine. We didn't have a dryer in those days. There was no heat, so whenever we had sub-zero temperatures, we had to bring the washing machine into the playroom so it wouldn't freeze up. In winter, we hung our clothes to dry on lines upstairs. West of the living room and kitchen was a hallway to the house's only bathroom. In it were a tub, sink, stool, and small cabinet.

Time spent around our kitchen table personified our life. You only had to partake in one meal with us to get a glimpse of the love our family shared. All were welcome, no matter if it was a buddy or two of ours, or a family friend or relative just dropping in. Any visit included friendly conversation, a treat, meal, some produce, flowers, or all of the above.

Dad built the family bench for the little kids when I was five or six. He nailed heavy two-by-sixes together with long spikes. The bench is six feet long and eleven inches wide, as long as the table. Almost sixty years later, it is still being used along the east wall. The youngest were relegated to the bench. We knew we were moving up in the world when someone left for college and we got promoted to a chair. Donna says she would like the bench someday. She would probably be entitled to it, considering she was the second youngest, and she and Beth used it more than anyone else.

At St. Sebastian's School, we always ate hot lunch. The head cook was Mrs. Wirtz, who always made great meals. When we got to high school, the cooking wasn't so great so we took our lunches. Most days Mark and I took three sandwiches plus cookies, chips, and a piece of fruit. With my meal I drank three cartons of milk. During wrestling season our lunches were much smaller so we could make our weight class. The girls didn't eat as much. Mom had twenty slices of bread on the table most mornings as she prepared our lunches. If we were short of ingredients, we would run to the trailer to see what Grandma had on hand. Three different years Mom and Dad had four students in high school. Later, the same four of us were in college at the same time. It might have been six, because Tom and Mike both attended college when they returned from hitches in the Army.

We always had someone visiting and everyone who came through our door felt welcome. With eleven kids living in our house, though, certain foods were usually rationed. Once my Uncle Al from North Carolina was our guest of honor for breakfast. I, as a little kid, informed him that he got only two pieces of bacon. Roxanne Biesack in Ellen's class had a sister in class with Mike and a brother Kevin in class with Mark and me. Roxanne said that the kids in her family decided if they ever ran away from home, they were going to hide out at the Muellers. Kevin said he wanted to live with us because we ate real butter.

Our freshman year in college, Mark brought home his friend Jerry for the weekend. Jerry was from a dairy in Sparta. To be polite, Mom asked, "How many eggs would you like?" Jerry replied, "I'll only take three." The look on Mom's face said, Mark! Why did you bring this glutton home? She asked the question to be courteous, not to learn how many eggs he usually ate for breakfast.

Mom made great apple pies, and she never followed a recipe when making them. Grandma would peel all the apples Mom needed. Mom knew if we snitched any dough because that was the only time she ever ran short. Oftentimes Mom's baked goods were going to a church bake sale, and we didn't get any. Today whenever I make a pie, I always make certain I keep some for myself. Audrey, after forty years, still smacks my hand with a wooden spoon when I try to steal batter or dough from any dessert she is making.

The playroom was where we stored all of our games and watched the three channels on our black-and-white television. CBS was Channel 2, NBC was Channel 4, and ABC was Channel 6. I don't know when we first got our television, but I remember it was a console style. If we didn't want to watch what was on, we went out to Grandma's trailer and watched television with her.

Our basement was under the whole house except the old kitchen on the south end. Dad decided he was going to dig it out and install ductwork, to heat it like the rest of the house. Dad and Jack Ramcke, a neighbor, used a small elevator to haul out the dirt they dug out, but they almost died of carbon monoxide poisoning from the engine exhaust. That project ended quickly.

At one time there was a stairway from the front room to the basement. I suppose before refrigeration, much of the food was stored in the basement, and having easy access was important. The stairs may have been taken out when the coal furnace was put in the house. When we were growing up there was just a door to nowhere on the north wall of Mom and Dad's bedroom. In the late 1970s when the bathroom was remodeled, that space behind the door is where the tub and shower were installed.

We kids wondered why shelves of canned goods sat in the basement for years. Mom explained that when she was first married, she had spent a long summer helping Grandma can food. At about that time, someone Mom knew died of food poisoning as a result of eating spoiled canned food. By then, freezers were popular so Mom froze vegetables instead. She never was a big proponent of canning.

We had a coal furnace in the basement until Mark and I were in high school. It sat beneath the kitchen and living room. On the north side of the house was our coal chute, where coal was dumped into a basement bin close to the furnace, making shoveling easier. In winter, coal was delivered to our house regularly. When we had a really cold weather, the coal bin was replenished more often. If the bin ever ran empty, we went to Cox's Farm Store for a few gunnysacks of coal to hold us over. Using a big scoop shovel, we took turns filling the hopper that fed the coal into the furnace. On cold nights the hopper had to be filled more frequently. Burning coal produced clinkers, an incombustible residue or irregular lump of what had been coal. We used a long rod with hooks to remove the clinkers whenever the furnace became full. We put them in a nonflammable metal basket to cool. We later put them on the driveway to fill any potholes we had. One night the coal furnace blew up, filling the house with black soot. Fortunately, Dad's friend Larry Rashlegger, jack-of-all-trades, was able to replace it with a new natural gas furnace.

Our steps going upstairs faced south. The stairs were really steep and the steps not very deep. In high school, whenever we came in late we always slipped in the back door, and we became experts at avoiding the squeaks as we crept up those old stairs. It was important not to wake Mom and Dad. Today, I am amazed at the coordination it takes to navigate these narrows steps while climbing straight up. It's almost like ascending a ladder; you need to use both your hands for balance.

At the top was a small landing and then straight on was the entrance to the attic. When we were kids at Easter and Halloween, we used to shoot dice against that door. Tom and Mike, the older brothers, would always win and take away Mark's and my candy.

We had four bedrooms upstairs. One little one at the top of stairs on the right belonged to Tom. You made a left and this was the hallway going north. To the right was Mike's room, bigger than Tom's. On the north were the two biggest rooms. The one straight ahead belonged to our sisters Mary, Ellen, and Jane. When Donna and Beth came along Tom and Mike were pretty much gone, so their two rooms were used by some of the rest of us. The room on the northwest we called the boys' room. Mark, Steve, Tim, and I slept there in bunk beds when we weren't camping north of the house or sleeping in the barn. We didn't have heat or air conditioning upstairs. We did have a grate that let heat come up through the floor on the north end of the hallway. We used a lot of blankets. In winter, the air in the house would get so dry. There was no such thing as a humidifier back then, so Mom would put cans of water upstairs to put moisture in the air. I don't think it ever helped much. The bedroom windows upstairs used to get a lot of frost on them in the bitter cold. I know in later years Mom used to have electric blankets on all the beds.

We lived only four miles from Lake Michigan, so most summer nights were pretty comfortable. Usually the breeze would come off the lake, dropping the temperature sometimes twenty to thirty degrees in an hour or two. On those nights dew soaked everything. Walking a few feet through the grass made your shoes look as if they had been soaked in a bucket of water. On the hot nights we did have, I remember sleeping with a wet washcloth on my stomach to cool off.

When we were little Mom used to always say, "It time for b-e-d." I knew it meant it was bedtime but I didn't know she was spelling "bed." I remember when Mom changed the sheets on our beds. First, she would put on the fitted sheet, and let us lie down. Then she would flutter the top sheet on top of us. That was fun for any preschooler.

We got all the childhood diseases. Mumps, chicken pox, measles, and German measles, the flu — we got them all. When one of us became sick, everyone came down with it. German measles was the best illness to get. There was no itching or pain and you got to stay home from school. By the time we reached high school, though, the importance of not missing school was pretty well engrained into us. If we got sick in high school we didn't want to stay home, because it was a hassle getting our homework caught up.

When I was two years old, I fell ten feet from the second floor of the granary. My brother Mike, age six, went up and I followed. With quite a sense of humor, he claims he pushed me. The fall required several stitches in my chin, from which I still carry a big scar. When I was five or six, Dad tore down the old granary, blacksmith shop, and a couple of other out-buildings just to the west of the drive on the back side of our yard. When we removed all the rubble there was a stone sticking out of the dirt. When we decided to dig it out we soon learned it was a boulder. My finger got in the way of someone's shovel, removing my nail. This was frightening for this little boy. It was a number of years before the rock was finally removed from the earth. It measured four feet by thirty inches high and thirty inches wide. It sat for years. Eventually Dad gave it to someone who asked for it. By the pound, what would that yard ornament be worth today?

Mark got burned two times. Once he stuck his hand in scalding water. He may still have the scar on the back of his hand. The second time, he pulled a hot coffeepot down on himself. That time Mom knew to put him in cold water. Mom said after the freezing bath, a layer of skin came off when she removed his shirt. There were no lasting scars from that mishap. Tim almost died from pneumonia at six months of age. Donna as a toddler got into some turpentine, which required a trip to the hospital.

We had a number of broken bones, but stitches and nail puncture wounds were the most common reasons for our trips to the doctor. Mom and Dad loved Doctor Scheller, a high school classmate of hers. He never prescribed expensive treatments unless absolutely necessary. Appointments didn't mean much to Doctor Scheller, either. He was a wonderful man who would treat everyone whether scheduled or not. We had long waits in the doctor's office. I remember one time I signed in for my school physical then went to bale hay. I came back three hours later, and the doctor was ready to see me.

We got our tonsils and adenoids out two or three at a time. Tom and Mike were together. Tom had his adenoids removed three times, so his third time he and Ellen went to the hospital together. Mark, Jane, and I all had ours out at the same time. Steve and Tim went together. I'm sure it was cheaper that way. I remember we got to eat all the ice cream we wanted. That was a once and only.

When we were kids we suffered from boils. They were similar to a big pimple, except a hundred times bigger. One summer I endured three of them. Once the boil got ripe, it was squeezed to remove the core. Only then would it heal and the pain go away. The problem was you didn't know when the core was ready to be removed. If you squeezed too soon, it was painful. In our desperation, we were willing to try almost anything to see improvement. Using a Coke bottle was one method we tried to remove the core. A bottle would be put in boiling water, and the opening at the top was stuck over the point of the boil. The suction it created was supposed to pull the garbage out of the boil. I don't know if this procedure ever actually worked, but it did leave a circular burn mark that added to our discomfort. Mom, desperate to end our boil plague, bought an automatic dishwasher with our sweet corn profits in the summer of 1965. We were probably one of the first in Kenosha to own one of these machines. It was a timesaver that also killed germs. Mom always overloaded the dishwasher and didn't rinse the dishes when loading. She believed that was the job of the dishwasher. Over the years Dad often complained that the dishes weren't clean. Her response always was, "The dishes are sterile, which makes them safer than if we did them by hand." She had a point; we never again had boils.

When Mom was a student at St. George's Grade School in Kenosha, the nuns always told the kids not to drink unpasteurized milk because it wasn't safe. Mom's family had a cow. Not wanting to die, she never drank much milk. When Mom bought a pasteurizer in 1963 or 1964, she was comforted knowing none of her kids would succumb to the ravages of bad milk. The milk pasteurizer heated the milk to one hundred forty-five degrees, killing all the germs in a two-gallon metal container. When the machine buzzed, we set the jug in the sink and ran cold water on the outside of the jug until the milk was cool. The milk was then poured into one-gallon glass jars and put in the refrigerator. We pasteurized only the milk we drank. Mom's milk customers bought raw unpasteurized milk. My wife, Audrey, and her family had an eighty-cow dairy herd, and they always drank raw milk with no bad results. I am thankful the nuns were wrong. To this day I am a big milk drinker.

Working in construction, Dad used to get a lot of used lumber left over from various jobs he worked. Knowing he fixed his own windows, people used to give him old glass windows to repair the many broken panes caused by our horsing around. Dad had a station for fixing windows in the basement. Much of the glass Dad used for replacement was very old. As glass ages it become brittle and breaks easily. With a lot of practice Dad became good at this job, but found it frustrating work. Some panes of glass required several attempts before he succeeded. That is the reason Dad used to get angry whenever we broke any windows in the house. I am surprised he never taught us to repair our own mistakes. Two of the window mishaps I remember involved Mark and me during a wrestling match and a golf challenge. Mike, being older, decided to wrestle the two of us no-handed, resulting in my crashing through the window of the front door. Then when Mark and I were in eighth or ninth grade we played a little golf. Of course, practice was required if we expected to improve. One day our competition was to see who could hit the ball farthest. Mark was the winner when he sent a beautiful drive into our bedroom window through two panes of glass. If the rules had included keeping the ball on the fairway, I would have won.

I have no idea how Mom and Dad kept us clothed. I have selective memory like my Dad. If something was bad, I often don't remember it. Here a few things I remember about clothes. Grandma used to put patches on our everyday clothes, mend, and sew on buttons. When we were little, iron-on patches were the fad. Mark and I had Huckleberry Hound or Yogi Bear on our knees. If we needed new shoes, Mom would get them for us. Because we knew money was tight, I remember putting cardboard in my shoes. It didn't work so well after a rain. Our Saturday evening ritual often included butchering a couple of chickens for Sunday dinner, as well as scraping mud and polishing everyone's good shoes for church in the morning.

Mom had a sanguine personality. She made fun out of many otherwise mundane events. She loved Christmas and was always abuzz about its preparations. When we were little, when she talked about Christmas presents in front of us she used to spell whatever she was talking about. Once we learned to spell and understood conversations, she would continue the same discussions, but would say, "I picked up that i-t-e-m." Throughout the Christmas season, until we received our presents, she continued to spell i-t-e-m every time we kids were within earshot. We always had a day off school December 8 because it was a Holy Day, the Feast of The Immaculate Conception. Three or four times, Mom took us to Milwaukee on the train Christmas shopping on that day. I am pretty sure this trip was for the train ride, not for the shopping. Mom always worked hard to give us experiences.

When we were growing up, we saved our money through the year and spent it all for Christmas presents. Giving to others was a big part of why this season was such an important part of our lives. Tom and Mike would shop on Christmas Eve day, come home during the late afternoon, and lock themselves in Mike's bedroom so they could play with the presents they were going to give us younger ones later. When supper was over, after the kitchen was in order, we kids would open the gifts we gave each other. We kids used to pool our money and give Mom and Dad one Christmas present. The first big one was the 1969 family photo, the one in the front of this book. It was taken when Mark and I were sophomores. I have mentioned that we all grew early, and by eighth grade we were all done growing. At that point we four oldest boys were about the same height. The photographer had Tom and Mike each stand on a brick, I guess to balance the photo, which made them appear taller. Another time we gave Mom and Dad our family's first color television.

Mom had a fun sense of humor. Before Dad raised his own trees, every Christmas Mom would purchase three trees. One was for Grandma, who stood it on a table in her trailer. Mom and Dad had one in the living room that held all the nice breakable ornaments. We kids had ours in the playroom adorned with many homemade creations. Always trying to get the best deal, she waited until a couple of days before Christmas to go tree hunting. The guys working at the tree lots used to hate to see her coming. Some would get so angry they threatened to throw the trees away before negotiating with her. When we were young, flocked trees were all the rage. I remember white and pink. We never got one of those; they were probably too expensive and messy. We never got the fancy ones. Mom reasoned that buying a tree late was okay, because they stayed fresh longer, and six of her seven sisters — all but one were local — never visited until after Christmas anyway. Plus, tradition didn't allow Catholics to take their tree down before the Feast of the Epiphany, January 6. Each sister made the circuit checking out each other's tree, sometimes with kids in tow, other times not. The visit gave each sister an opportunity to admire her sibling's holiday efforts, have coffee, eat cookies, and gossip.

We older kids always went to Midnight Mass for Christmas. One time after Tom and Mike were able to drive, we returned from Midnight Mass in a blizzard. Weather forecasts back then weren't made as they are today. If Mom and Dad had known a storm was approaching, they never would have let us leave the house that night. Fortunately, we got home safely. The original St. Sebastian Church was tiny. We sometimes went to Saint Bonaventure Seminary in Sturtevant to Midnight Mass. It was never crowded, and the church had beautiful stained glass windows and a beautiful service. Once we were deemed old enough, that was long after we knew about Santa, we were permitted to stay up late and go to Midnight Mass. The tenderfoot Mass-goer was then designated Santa's new helper. It was his or her job to find the presents Mom had hidden all over the farm. They were everywhere, in the trunk of the car, the pump house, the old shanty, old kitchen, the attic. Sometimes toys required simple assembly, or so the instructions said. Each Christmas, it became clearer to me that I was never going to pursue a career in any field that required mechanical skills. I have five brothers, and three of them can put together or fix pretty much anything. Two of them are mechanically challenged. I am somewhere in between.

Christmas morning was magic. Santa's gifts were always unwrapped. Our playroom was always wall-to-wall presents. To this day it amazes me how Mom ever kept track of who got what. We used to wake early and pester until Mom and Dad would let us get up. We were always up by 5 a.m. I recently heard the story about one time someone was stalled or stuck along Highway 31 at 3:30 a.m. one cold Christmas morning. At that hour they were fearful until they saw our farmhouse lights. Soon Dad had them on their way.

For kids raised in a Catholic family, Christmas and Easter were important religious holy days, not just holidays. Easter preparations were enhanced with new dresses, pressed pants and shirts. After church we were lined up from oldest to youngest for photographs. Today we can tell the date of each photo by determining how old the youngest in the picture was.

The Easter basket hunt was a significant part of our Easter celebration. On Saturday night we were asked the degree of difficulty with which we wanted our baskets hidden. The choices were medium, difficult, or impossible. We boys would usually choose option No. 3. How stupid. Sometimes our search took hours. Anyone still looking in the afternoon was assisted with the "You're getting warmer" method of finding hidden treasure. I remember a few places baskets were hidden: in trees, in the pump house, on the house roof, in the basement up on a ledge behind the locked door that once led to the front room, and hanging under the cistern cover in the back yard. Our Easter basket when finally found was like the rainbow's pot of gold. It was chock full of jacks, a bouncy ball, a new pair of tennis shoes, and lots of candy. Unfortunately, our candy was soon lost to my older brothers Tom and Mike in a shrewd game of dice we played against the attic door at the top of the stairs. On those days candy was legal tender. I don't know what Tom and Mike used for currency, but when we were done they always had plenty.

Along with Easter, All Saints Day, the day after Halloween, was also a holy day. We were off school for both, and our candy never lasted too long on either day. I'm pretty sure Mom didn't know we were gambling on these religious holy days.

Another Easter ritual was Dad digging up the field tile. In the spring when the snow melted, our sewer wouldn't drain properly. Dad would have to spend a couple of days digging trenches locating the plugged tile.

Then he would clean the obstruction in the tile with a drain snake to make the water flow again. When the new city sewer system was installed along Highway 31, our house was hooked into it. They said Dad was so happy he spent the whole first day flushing the toilet, knowing he was never again going to spend Easter Sunday digging holes.

Mom always made a big deal out of celebrating holidays, holy days, and our birthdays. She majored in making everyone feel important on his or her special day. She made it special by baking two cakes. The birthday boy or girl chose the flavor of one, and she decided on the other. Our choices were chocolate, marble, or banana. The cake of our choice was ablaze with candles while everyone in the family sang "Happy Birthday." The cake always had candles to signify our age, and it was served with ice cream. I'm sure our presents weren't too costly for Mom and Dad, but they were special.

St. Sebastian's had an auction as a fundraiser on two of my birthdays while in high school. These were a Saturday and a Sunday. Even at that age I was disappointed that my birthday wasn't the priority. Growing up, we never celebrated our birthday with friends. With a big family that would have been impossible. I do remember that we had a day on the farm with our friends on at least a couple of occasions while we still attended Holy Trinity.

One Saturday Tom and Mike invited several of their friends out. They had a nice picnic lunch then spent the day doing all the fun things kids do on a farm. They ate, played softball, and explored the woods, creek, and barn. On another weekend, Mary, Ellen, Mark, Jane, and I invited some of our friends to do the same. After a while we didn't have these parties anymore; maybe we just figured we were always inviting cousin or friends to stay overnight anyway. At least, we boys did.

Of all the board games we played growing up, Monopoly was at the top of the list. In our house, cards were even more important. When we were little we played Concentration, 500 Rummy, and Tripoli. When Mom thought we were ready, she taught us all how to play 500, a fun game played by four people.

Once we mastered 500, it was on to Schafkopf, known as Sheepshead, a German card game. Mom loved it, and she also loved going to the casino.

The following is a typical Mom story. Joanne (Thom) Ramcke lived her teen years across the road, and babysat for Mom regularly. She was four years older than Tom, the oldest in our family. Her whole adult life she has lived on KR west of the creek, about a quarter mile from our farm.

She recently shared the following story. It was probably sometime in the mid-1990s; all of us kids were grown and gone. A snowstorm hit one night. In the morning, Dad refused to get the tractor out to clear the drive.

Joanne got a desperate call from Mom asking for a favor.

"Could you give me a ride to Racine?" Mom begged.

"I can try," Joanne said. When Joanne arrived, Mom was standing in snow almost to her waist next to her suitcase, which was sitting on a snow bank.

They proceeded north on Highway 31 hoping the drifts by Richard School weren't too deep to plow through. Eventually they arrived at the Regency Mall on Highway 11 where an anxious bus driver was waiting to transport a load of passengers to the Menominee Casino and Resort in Keshena.

Because Mom was the coordinator of many of these jaunts up north, the bus driver often would pick her up at the farm. I guess during blizzards he drove only on the main highways.

Below are two more examples, near the end of Mom's life, of Mom just being Mom.

Jane took Mom, age ninety-three, to the emergency room one Friday morning in October 2015. Her blood count was low, and she needed a transfusion. The whole time Mom kept looking at the clock. She was discharged about noon, but Jane, an avid Sheepshead player herself, refused to take Mom to a Sheepshead game that afternoon. Dad would have gone ballistic.

The following month, while Mom spent Friday and Saturday in the hospital, Donna came down from Marshall to stay with Dad at the farm. Mary was coming for the week to care for Dad and Mom while Mom recovered.

When Mom was released at 5 p.m. Sunday, she already had her plan in mind. She figured Mary could give her a ride to her Scrabble game Monday afternoon. Again, it was Jane who decided Mom couldn't play. If she had, Mary in her frustration would have gone back home to DePere.

Mom loved people and was always looking for an event or a party to go to. She celebrated life right to the end.

Before Mom and Dad ever met, both of their fathers played Schafkopf together. To this day, our family still plays Schafkopf once a month at the farm with cousins and friends. Dad played 500, but not Sheepshead; his favorite game was *Cribbage*.

Dad's real love, however, was travel. About ten years before Dad died, he was taking a trip to Canada and Alaska with Mary and her husband, Mark Reinhart. After 9/11, our government got much stricter about passport requirements. Dad needed a new one, so he sent to the state capital in Madison for a copy of his birth certificate.

There was no record of a George Edwin Mueller born in Wisconsin. After some searching, it was discovered Dad's real name was Victor George Edwin Mueller. His whole life, he never knew.

Chapter 6: The Three R's plus Religion

Catholic education was important to my parents. Their sacrifices yielded a bumper crop. They were proud of their children and the fact we all took the opportunity to get an education. Growing up, Mom attended St. George's Catholic Grade School in Kenosha, Wisconsin. Then she and Dad both graduated from St. Catherine High School in Racine, Wisconsin. Mom and Dad were parishioners at St. Sebastian's Church in Sturtevant. This was the church my Grandfather Peter Mueller helped build and where he was a charter member. When my oldest brother Tom, six years older than I am, was ready to start first grade, St. Sebastian parish didn't yet have a school. Holy Trinity Parish in Racine had a Catholic grade school, so our family joined that parish. Mom and Dad knew that the nuns would give us a good education and make sure we behaved. Thus began our nine years as members of Holy Trinity.

When I started first grade, I struggled mightily. Even though I wasn't learning, they passed me because I was so cute. Second grade was pretty much the same story. They agreed to pass me, but only if I attended summer school. During this time someone came up with the bright idea that maybe I was struggling because of poor eyesight. So, I wore glasses for the next year or two. Shouldn't a professional eye doctor have been able to tell if a little kid could see or not?

Two of the years we attended Holy Trinity, six of us kids had to run a quarter of a mile every morning to catch the bus. It stopped at the corner, the intersection of Highway 31 and KR County Line Road. The first year Tom was in eighth grade, the second year Tom was a freshman at Saint Cat's, and Mike, now a seventh grader, was responsible for getting us all there on time. Jane was now the first grader. I remember on several occasions, regardless of the weather, Mike sprinted the 440 yards with

Jane under his arm so we wouldn't miss the bus. That might explain why Mike became a good athlete when he got to high school.

On bad weather days when the buses wouldn't start, Father Labaj would drive out and pick us up for school. There is no telling how many kids he was able to sardine into his car, before seatbelts.

During the summer of 1961, I spent mornings in school. It was horrible. I missed out on swim lessons, and the only thing I learned all summer was to stay away from the bully at recess. He was a year older than I was, wore flashy clothes and, like me, had blond hair and a crew cut. Today we call those buzz cuts. At the end of each day's torturous classroom session, Mom would pick me up and rush me over to the pool where my brothers and sisters were taking their swim lessons. I had only ten or fifteen minutes to splash in the water while waiting for my siblings to finish. I was deprived of pool time while everyone else, I thought, was having so much fun. You know how when you can't have something you want it even more? That might explain my lifelong love of swimming. To this day I swim and run in the water at our local YMCA three miles a week. That traumatic summer did not prepare me for third grade, though, and who knows how much damage it did to this eight-year-old's self-esteem.

Every kid in our school was afraid of my third grade teacher. She could have played the supporting role in the classic movie *Wizard of Oz* — remember the unpleasant Witch from the West who rode the bicycle? My teacher lifted her students in and out of their desks by pulling on their ear. Not only was this embarrassing, it hurt like h_ _ _. Her teaching methods were much different from my first grade and second grade teachers, both nuns, who were loving mother hens. This teacher's punishment was administered for several crimes including, but definitely not limited to, failing to do your homework, misbehaving, and not learning. I am amazed my ears aren't bigger today than they are, because I made frequent trips to and from my desk for all three of these infractions. I remember once being assigned a five-hundred-word theme for not having my homework done. It was due the very next day. Being the typical eight-year-old, I didn't tell Mom or Dad until after my Cub Scout meeting at 9 p.m.

That night I stayed up well past my normal bedtime. My oldest brother, Tom, a freshman in high school, was drafted to help me compose my paper. He told me what to write, and I wrote in my own script. This assignment for Tom was tough because I couldn't spell, and he had to keep waking me up. My hand hurt so badly, I was sure it was going to fall off. As it turns out this was good practice, because a couple of years later I started milking our Guernsey cow. Then both of my hands felt like they were going to break. We finished late, never quite reaching five hundred words, but it was accepted anyway.

After third grade, when I still couldn't read, the school decided I was going to repeat third grade. Back then, repeating a grade was called failing or flunking, because that is what it was. Looking back, I think my problem was slow maturation. Maybe being born three weeks premature in 1953 had something to do with it. I'm pretty sure anyone who knew me back then would never have predicted I was going to become a good athlete, a teacher for more than forty years, and an avid reader and writer. As it turned out, flunking third grade was one of the best things that ever happened to me. In today's politically correct world, no one would ever call it failing because it might harm someone's self-esteem. The truth is that you don't grow in life without some failure, and self-esteem improves only when you succeed. This I eventually did. In my opinion, one of the biggest mistakes parents make is never letting their children fail. Today, we see the results of this all the time. How many millennials are still living in Mom and Dad's basement? And how often do grandparents have to raise their grandkids? Mom and Holy Trinity's head priest didn't see eye to eye, and she didn't approve of my third grade teacher's corporal punishment. My flunking gave my folks a good reason for returning to St. Sebastian, which now had a Catholic grade school. They did feel bad, however, to leave behind many friends they had established over those nine years.

Going back to St. Sebastian's gave Mom and Dad a chance to reconnect with old friends and parishioners. The switch also gave me a fresh start, where people didn't know of my early educational deficiencies. At St. Sebastian's the classes were already overcrowded, but with Grandma Mary's connections Mom was able to get all six of us enrolled. Mark and I were now classmates and would go through school together for the next ten years. Every class probably had more than forty kids. Mary remembers that Jane's second grade class alone had sixty students.

Several years later, Mark and I attended colleges only twenty-five miles apart. We graduated on the same day, May 8, 1976 — I from Loras College in Dubuque, Iowa, at 11 a.m. and Mark from University of Wisconsin-Platteville at 2 p.m. One year later my best friend John McLean graduated from Loras at 11 a.m. and my wife, Audrey, and my sister Jane graduated from Platteville at 2 p.m. To this day I don't enjoy graduation ceremonies.

When we arrived at St. Sebastian's, Mike was in eighth grade, Mary in sixth, Ellen in fifth, and Mark and I in third. Many people over the years thought Mark and I were twins because we were in the same grade. Jane was in second grade. That year Steve was at the local public school in kindergarten. He was the first in our family to attend school before first grade. Tim, two years younger than Steve, was born in 1959. Donna was born in 1964, and Beth, the youngest, made her appearance in 1966.

Mike belonged to the Catholic Youth Organization (CYO), which once a month sponsored a roller skating party. On Tuesday nights we used to ride the school bus up to Milwaukee to skate. It was difficult learning to skate, but once you figured it out skating was a ball.

At Holy Trinity I had struggled through first, second, and third grades. At St. Sebastian's, grades three through five were tough, but kind of a blur academically. I do remember that we had five boys named John in our class, and it was enjoyable having Mark in the same class. I didn't know it at the time, but having that extra year in grade school helped better prepare me for sixth grade.

Recess was pretty important. We used to play roundup, palm-palm-pull-away, red rover, and softball, and in winter we would skate on the pond behind school.

In sixth grade, I had a young hot teacher, Miss Andrea Aiello. In those days, a woman could teach after two years of college. Because she had a fall birthday, Miss Aiello started teaching at age nineteen. With her choleric and sanguine temperament, she was tough but fun, and we all loved her. Her positive expectations and remedial reading helped Mark and me to begin succeeding in school. Miss Aiello was Jane's teacher the following year, and later, Jane sang at Miss Aiello's wedding. Who knows where I might be today if I had been passed to the next grade level without the extra reading help from someone like Miss Aiello. What would have happened to me if teachers had kept passing me even though I had difficulty reading?

Today in many schools, students continue to be moved on even when they aren't learning. If students aren't learning, how is a high school diploma preparing them for the world of work?

St. Sebastian's School had two buses: the big bus, which held sixty-six students, and the little bus with a capacity of fifty-four. These numbers were assuming you could fit three kids in a seat. Our school ran two routes before and after school, for a total of eight each day. It switched each month. If you were on the first route, you got to school an hour early, and attended Mass every morning. At the end of the day, the bus left right after school. If you were on the second route, school started immediately upon your arrival. Then you had an hour wait after school before leaving. If you were on the late route and you finished your homework, you were allowed to go out and play. Back in the 1960s there were mountains of snow each winter, which made for some great King of the Mountain games to the south of school. The good thing was that when we started at St. Sebastian's, we caught the bus right in front of our house, and we were among the last to board the bus each morning. If we were on the late route, we got to sleep in an extra hour. Then after school, we did homework. At night the second route was horrible. By the time we got home, two hours after school had dismissed, the bus was almost empty. It seemed as if we were on the bus that whole time. We were almost the last off, and wouldn't you know, we were always on the second route in the spring when the warm weather hit. What torture.

One spring day while I was in fifth grade, I had to stay to finish my homework and then I was supposed to ride the second bus home. I didn't want to wait so I decided to walk. It took much longer than I expected. Thinking I could save some time, I tried to cut through our muddy field. About two hundred yards from the house I was feeling pretty sorry for myself when I spotted our bus driving by. Occasionally in the warm weather we would ride our bikes to and from school. One windy afternoon the four-mile trip took only fifteen minutes. At the time we thought that was quite a feat for our one-speed bikes.

In fifth or sixth grade, Mark and I began serving Mass. Once we became altar boys, we quickly forgot all the prayers and learned to mumble at all the proper places during Mass. Steve "Mouchy" Thomas, a friend, was the only one who ever really cared enough to take his altar boy duties seriously. One friend used to sample the wine when we servers were preparing for Mass. It must have been pretty watered down, because I don't ever remember any mishaps during the service. Mark and I served at the 6:30 a.m. Mass on Sundays.

In sixth grade, Mark and I started figuring out how to be successful in school. We were pretty good athletes, which helped our social standing among our classmates. Either in sixth or seventh grade, Mark and I took Grandma's Wisconsin Territory map to school for Show and Tell. It was an eight-foot canvas map from 1846. I believe it was in the attic of our house in the 1890s when Grandpa Mueller moved in. Grandma later donated the map to the Hyslop Foundation in the late 1960s. Another time we took a quart of cream from our Guernsey cow to school to demonstrate how butter was made. Starting at the front of the room, each student gave the jar a few good shakes then passed it to the next person. When it got to the end of the room, it was butter.

In seventh grade we started switching classrooms with a couple of great teachers. We had Miss Rondon, a classmate of my Dad's when they were young. Sister Thomas Mary was our principal, but she also taught a fun music class. We sang the *Mary Poppins* songs and also a lot of modern religious songs for Mass because the Catholic Church was starting to implement some of the changes that came about from Vatican Council II. Sister thought I had a good voice, but I never pursued music because it wasn't cool. She herself wasn't much over thirty. When we got to St. Catherine's in ninth grade we had her younger sister Jane as a classmate. In eighth grade, Sister Ramone was added to the staff. Though nearing retirement, she was one of the neatest teachers I ever had. She understood middle-schoolers as well as anyone I have ever known.

We still had recess in eighth grade. This was pretty important because we didn't have physical education. Each time the boys or girls got in trouble, the other group would get an extended time outdoors while the perpetrators were talked to. I taught eighth graders for thirty-four years. Today more than ever I believe recess is really important. It would help our students be more physically active, helping to burn off excess energy and weight. Maybe fewer kids would need meds. Where I taught, it seemed that our school's office was a pharmacy with all the drugs that were dispensed each day.

Some of the girls in our class thought our parties would be enhanced if the boys knew how to dance. Donna, Patty, Mary Lou, Cindy, Cathy, Nancy, Evelyn, and Julie harangued Sister Ramone until she relented. From then on some of our recess time became designated dance practice time. The girls taught the boys this important life lesson.

Today I don't dance much if I can help it, but I will never forget "The Letter" by the Box Tops, which came out in 1967; to this day it is still one of my all-time favorite songs. The one dance I do enjoy is the polka, but we weren't taught that at recess.

Our class had a bunch of boy-girl parties — some sanctioned by parents, others not. Mark and I knew better than to even ask for permission to go to those without chaperones. I recently saw Donna Celeste, my classmate, whose mother and I are second cousins. She commented on how bad our class was. I really didn't remember that we were. She was probably making reference to some of our scandalous co-ed parties in eighth grade. I remember spin-the-bottle was pretty popular. It couldn't have been any worse than my sister's class. She said, "In our class we had more kids who didn't graduate from high school than the number who went to college."

We couldn't have been that depraved, or our teachers wouldn't have taken us on three outings that spring. We took a religious foray to Holy Hill. Maybe they figured this was their last chance to get us to consider a religious vocation. In our class, I'm pretty sure there aren't any ordained priest or sisters. Another outing was the all-school picnic at Petrifying Springs Park, which was a mile from our home.

Our eighth-grade class trip was to Muskego Beach amusement park on my fifteenth birthday. That day the police pulled our bus over. Apparently, Larry had been on some rides that didn't agree with him. He puked into several tissues and was disposing of them out the window. Even back then, that was environmentally unacceptable.

As altar boys, Mark and I had to learn all the prayers in Latin, then later relearn them in English. Because the prayers were difficult to remember, at a young age we learned how to cram. This was a skill that was going to prove to be pretty valuable later when we reached college. The old St. Sebastian's Church, of which my Grandfather Peter Mueller was a charter member, was so small we had four Masses each Sunday morning. They were at 6:30 a.m., always a low Mass; 8:30 a.m.; 10 a.m.; and noon. Whenever we entered church, we learned to count how many candles were lit on the altar. If there were only two, it was a Low Mass and was going to be only thirty minutes. When the altar was ablaze with several candles, this meant a High Mass that would be a whole hour. For centuries the Mass had always been said in Latin. The priest would face the altar, with his back to the faithful. After the Vatican II Council in the early 1960s, priests started saying Mass in English, facing the congregation. This is also when the churches started offering Saturday night Masses as an option to attending on Sunday.

One of the servers would ring the bells when the priest raised the consecrated host and the wine. Some servers would see how long they could ring the bells before getting a dirty look from the priest. To receive Communion, everyone would kneel along the kneelers in front of the sanctuary. When distributing Communion, the priest put the host onto each person's tongue, and said, "Body of Christ." Most men receiving Communion would respond with, "Ah-men." Most women said, "Ay-men." The altar boy held the paten, a little plate with a handle, under the parishioner's chin. They had to pay attention that the priest didn't drop the host and that they didn't accidentally smack the parishioner in the throat. If the host was dropped, it was supposed to land on the paten and not on the floor. I saw that happen only once and it took some time for the priest to properly clean up three dropped hosts. After receiving Communion, the recipient would get up and someone else knelt to receive. The priest was the only one who distributed Communion back then. Using the paten and kneeler made distributing Communion a much slower process than it is today.

Sometimes we would attend Mass at St. Peter's on the edge of Kenosha if the Mass time was more convenient than our church's. Apparently, St. Peter's had problems with people leaving after Communion, before the service was complete. Someone's brilliant answer was to put up a sign at the back of church, which everyone could read on the way out. The sign read, JUDAS WAS THE FIRST TO LEAVE! I bet that really made parishioners want to attend weekly Mass. Maybe making church a more welcoming environment, or improving the priest's message, would have worked better in keeping people until the end of Mass.

When Mark and I arrived at St. Catherine's High School, at first we enjoyed the social life of high school far more than the academic responsibilities. I remember freshman year, after report cards came home. "Would you prefer to go to Bradford Public High School in Kenosha?" Dad admonished. "If your grades don't improve, you will!" We both got on the ball and never again had that discussion at home.

At St. Catherine's, boys' athletics were big. Girls' sports didn't start until 1972, the fall after Mark and I graduated. Jane was the captain on St. Cat's first girls' basketball team. The four years Mark and I were at St. Cat's, our school won eight state championships. Four titles were in cross country with the individual champion in four out of five years. They had two state championships in basketball, and one each in baseball and wrestling.

Our freshman year, there were twelve hundred students at St. Cat's. Very few were farm kids. Wrestling was still a young program at our school. My brother Mike was on one of the first teams. Even though he did well, his team got almost no press, and practice facilities were meager. At the time, our varsity basketball team was a perennial contender for the state championship.

St. Catherine's wasn't in the greatest neighborhood. They had some problems with vandalism and break-ins. Their solution was to buy Brutus, the Doberman Pinscher guard dog. His handler was Mr. Fisher, the longtime custodian. Even before Mr. Fisher retired, Kevin Hogan, one of our classmates, took on some responsibilities for Brutus. When Brutus died, they bought a replacement that also did a good job of keeping out intruders.

There were a lot of nuns who taught at St. Catherine's. They all loved our family because Grandma, Mom, and Dad for years had given apples to their convent in the fall. It also didn't hurt that Tom, Steve, and all of my sisters were very good students.

When we were in high school 1968 to 1972, we thought Sister Albina was ancient. She was our attendance officer at St. Catherine's. She was about four feet tall, and everyone was afraid of her. Anytime you missed school, you were to call Sister Albina in the attendance office to report your absence. Senior year Mark, Phil Fellner, and Mike Chiappe skipped school. They went up to Mitchell Field, the Milwaukee Airport, to play arcade games. The plan was to call school pretending to be each other's parent. Phil called first: "Hello, this is Mr. Chiappe. Mike is sick and won't be at school today." Sister Albina said, "Could you spell your last name for me, please?" Phil didn't know how to spell Mike's last name. Sister said, "I know this isn't Mr. Chiappe. Who is this?" After Phil hung up, Mike said to Mark, "It's my turn to call for you." Mark replied, "No, that's okay, I'll take my chances."

After a couple of hours of arcade games, they had to pay the parking fee before they could leave the lot. While Mike was reaching for some money, his foot slipped off the brake. The car started rolling and instead of hitting the brake, he accidentally accelerated — breaking off the tollgate.

Whenever we arrived at school tardy from the farm, more often than we should have, Sister Albina always let us go to class without any penalty. Jane saw her grave recently and learned that Sister Albina wasn't nearly as old as everyone had guessed. She died in 1988, and lived almost to ninety. We thought that was her age twenty years earlier.

Mom shared this story just a couple of years ago. Freshman year Mark was having a conflict with one of his teachers. Once she found out whose family he was part of, they got along much better. Sophomore year I just didn't get geometry. I dropped it midyear and did fine when I later took it as a junior. Even though I didn't study much, Sister Michaelina loved me in German class freshman year. Thankfully, with two years, I wasn't required to take a language in college. I think Sister Carolyn passed me in chemistry when I agreed to drop at semester.

Donna went to St. Catherine's for one year. She had friends she played softball with in Somers Township and decided she was going to switch schools. She completed her last three years at St. Joseph's. Beth, who was two years behind Donna, went all four years to St. Joseph's.

Dad hauled logs and firewood for Mark. The bridal wreath bushes behind him were one of Mom's favorites and a great place for kids to play hide-and-seek.

Mark and I and our siblings built fantastic snow forts behind the bridal wreath bushes around the side porch.

Chapter 7: Oh, the Trouble Kids Can Get Into

One time we were playing Tiger. Mark was the hunter, I was the prey. We must have been about seven. He threw a burdock spear at me and missed, but Steve was hit above the ear. That game ended suddenly with a trip to the doctor for stitches. Looking back, I am amazed we all, especially Mark and I, lived to adulthood. We had many adventures on and off the farm growing up. The most dangerous were operating the many farm implements, playing in the flooded creek, and diving from forty feet into the quarry.

Mike remembers being spanked twice while growing up: once for painting his little sister Mary, and the second time for firing off a shotgun in her direction. At ages four and six, Mike and Tom of course wanted to help Mom when she was painting the picnic table in the backyard with oil-based paint. This was back before we knew lead paint could harm you. Mom went into the house to answer the phone. This was almost fifty years before cell phones, and people had landlines, which at the time were usually a party line. A short time later when Mom returned, Mary, age two, was now picnic-table green. Mom was angry. After paddling both boys, she put Mary in the tub and scrubbed her with steel wool and kerosene to remove the paint. Thankfully, no scars remain from this trauma. Today Mary is probably the smartest of us kids, though two of my brothers would disagree because they are convinced *they* are the smartest.

The other spanking occurred a little later after Mike, age four, almost shot his little sister Mary, who was two. Tom was at school, in first grade at the time. The kid who lived across the road I will call an Eddie Haskell type after the mischievous character in *Leave It To Beaver*. According to Mom and Dad, this kid was a little hellion. He was older than Tom, but for some reason he wasn't in school that day.

Dad, at age ninety-eight, told his side of this story: "I was blamed for leaving my shotgun accessible to the kids. They snuck my 16-gauge shotgun from the house, then stole the shells from the upper cabinet shelf in the milk house." The boys took the gun and ammunition to the cow barn. "Eddie" helped Mike load the gun, then talked him into firing it. The recoil knocked Mike to the floor, and the blast hit the inside of the cow barn door. Mary, who had followed them, was just on the other side of that door. Eddie, seeing what he had caused, slipped through the back door and ran home. The explosion and Mary's screams brought Mom running. When Mom saw Mike out cold lying on the floor, she was certain her little boy had gone to heaven. Thankfully, three years later Joanne Thom Ramcke and her parents, Earl and Ruth, moved in across the road. Earl and Ruth lived there the remainder of their lives.

Mom always loved bridal wreath, the flowers she used in her wedding in 1946, which grew all along the south side of our wrap-around porch. They are pretty for a few days each spring, and a pain the rest of the year. They weren't always trimmed properly, so when they bloomed they hung over the porch, blocking the path. When they were touched, a thousand tiny petals fell. Anyone who unfortunately brushed against them after a Saturday night rain picked specks off his clothes all the way to church Sunday morning. Mom also loved lilacs, which to this day still stand north of the house. About twenty-five years ago, Dad decided he was tired of the lilacs for some reason. With his tractor, he ripped out the monster bush that stood near where Grandma's trailer used to be. Mom was so upset she didn't talk to him for weeks. It almost caused a divorce.

We always had those ugly juniper bushes in front of our living room and kitchen. They made great camouflage for our various yard games we played. The problem was we always got so scratched up whenever we used these for a hiding place.

If you have ever seen any of our early family photos, most were set up the same way. Mom took pictures of us only when we were clean. So on Sundays after church, she would line us up in the front yard, with the house as our backdrop. We were always dressed neatly and standing in the order of our age. Tom would be the first in line, and whoever was youngest at the time was on the opposite end. To this day anyone can figure out what year the picture was taken. It was always in the warmer months, and we would just look to see how old the one on the end was. Donna says that by the time she and Beth came along, Mom no longer did the lineup photos. They were toddlers when Tom and Mike had left home, and Mom wouldn't have been able to get any of us teenagers to pose. Looking at these old photos, my children noticed that more than once I was studying my watch while the photo was taken. I have always been very aware of time. Usually when I do a task, I know how long it will take. Often when we travel going from Iowa to Wisconsin or returning, I can predict to the minute when we will arrive.

Kick the Can was one of our favorite games growing up. We would set a big can in the middle of the front yard. One person was It. His or her goal was to catch everyone before any of them could kick the can. If they succeeded, It freed everyone who had been caught. When you spotted someone you ran to the can, placed your hand on top, and said "One, two, three, I caught _ _ _ _ _." To start the game, the person who was It would cover his eyes and count to twenty-five. Everyone else would run and hide. Most people would go behind the house. Others would hide in the scratchy juniper bushes in front of the house. Sometimes a brave soul would try to sneak behind the big tree or the double tree. These were the big old soft maple tree and the big poplar tree out by the road. We had to be able to run fast and gutsy to win at this game. Being slower was always frustrating for the younger kids, who were never able to win. The game usually ended abruptly when the loser stomped off crying. At this point it was time to try a different game.

Around the Moon was another of the games we played. The south wall of the pump house was always goal. The person who was It would create a punishment. Maybe you would have to go to the road and count five blue cars, or maybe you would have to run to the woods one hundred yards away. Then the person who was It would cover his face while someone else would say, "Around the moon, around the moon, someone poke this big fat goon," drawing a circle on the person's back with his finger. Then someone else would poke them inside the circle. They had to guess who poked them. If they were right, the poker was It. If they guessed wrong, then the original player was still It. Whoever was It had to do the punishment. While they were gone, everyone else would find a hiding place. When It returned, each person tried to hit the south wall of the pump house without first being seen. The goal of the person who was It was to spot each person, then tap the wall and call off their name. The first one caught would be It for the next round.

Of all the games we played as kids, croquet was the most dangerous. How Mom and Dad could ever have allowed us to play I don't understand. Most of us were pretty competitive, and really didn't appreciate losing legitimately. It was even worse when an opponent cheated. I remember on several occasions the culprits, usually the older kids, being chased by an enraged younger sibling trying to take them out with their croquet mallet. It's a good thing that with age comes more speed, or else these battles would have necessitated even more trips to the emergency room. Whenever these altercations occurred, it was always the signal for the conclusion to that day's croquet match.

Badminton could be played only if it wasn't windy. We used to play singles or doubles in a clearing east of the barn, between the orchard and our ball diamond. Our court was placed where it wouldn't interfere with our frequent ball games. Because we had no line judges, we built boundaries. By pounding stakes in the ground, then tying twine or string to them, we had an official-looking court. Knowing where out-of-bounds was helped to eliminate most fighting. We were older and a bit less impulsive when we played badminton. At that point we no longer tried to maim the victor when we lost. It is a good thing, because a racket is a more dangerous weapon: It is easier to swing with better accuracy than a croquet mallet.

Our horseshoe pits were south of our ball diamond between the badminton courts and the barn. Some summers we played a lot of horseshoes. We had permanent pits officially the correct distance apart. Wins were pretty important.

In the cow pasture we had a cow tank across the drive from the back yard. It was about eight feet long and thirty inches wide and tall. We didn't have air conditioning, so to cool off, we would fill the tank with water and play in it. It held three or four comfortably. On really hot days it always exceeded official capacity. When the tank leaked, we inserted a piece of inner tube, bolt and nut in the hole. Usually that would do the trick, as long as we kept adding more water.

We never had a riding mower. I guess we should be thankful that our mowers always had motors and weren't the rotary kind. We were fortunate there was a lawn mower shop just south of the restaurant. This made it easier to keep our push mowers running. We used to mow the front, back, south of the drive, and some years part of the orchard. When we did, that made it at least two acres to mow. That might be why even with a rider mower, to this day I don't enjoy mowing.

We played a lot of softball on the farm. Home plate and first base were just west of the current north end of Dad's apple orchard. With siblings, neighbors, and friends we could sometimes get ten to twelve kids for a game. As we got older, right field was off limits. A good hit would interfere with the traffic on Highway 31, so it was an out. Plus, with right field off limits, we could play with far fewer players. We could probably get a game up with as few as six people if we had to. We sometimes had one person pitch to both teams, requiring fewer fielders.

As young kids we worked at throwing a softball all the way over the roof of the barn, which was thirty-five feet tall and thirty-seven feet wide. Once we were able to get the ball over the top, we played catch over the barn. With one person in the front and one in the back, we probably didn't catch too many balls before they landed on the ground. When we were little we also played First Bounce or Fly. A novice with the bat attempted to throw a ball in the air and hit it to the other beginners in the field, who tried catching it. The first person to catch the ball either on the fly or on one bounce without dropping it became the new batter. Once we got older and could hit and catch better, we graduated to a game of 500 points. The batter hit the ball to the fielders, who accumulated points with each successful catch. A one-handed fly ball caught was worth 200 points, a two-handed fly ball caught was 100. A one-bounce was worth 75, two-bounce 50, and a grounder 25 points. If you missed a catch, the corresponding points were deducted from your score. The first player to reach 500 points became the new hitter.

If we didn't have enough for two full teams, we would play Scrub Up or Work Up. This game was played with two or three batters and everyone else was a fielder. The fielders progressed through the outfield to the infield, then to the pitcher. If the lead runner couldn't get to home plate, he was out and had to go play in the outfield. If the batter was called out, the other base runners stayed on base waiting for the pitcher, who now became the new batter they hoped would get them home safely. One time a neighbor boy Brett, known as Chipper, broke his collarbone sliding into second base. That was back before Pete Rose taught everyone the proper way to slide headfirst. We once put an old bedspring behind home plate to serve as a backstop. It didn't help much with errant pitches and throws.

There were three big trees north of Grandma's trailer. Before we ever had an official tent, we would string a rope between trees, drape blankets over it, and make ourselves a tent. Mark and I spent a lot of nights sleeping in our pup tent. One summer we slept in the tent every night for three weeks. Kevin Young joined us. He was often called our twelfth sibling, because he spent more time at our house growing up than at his own home. When we were still really young, we frequently zipped two sleeping bags together for warmth and all three of us boys would sleep that way all night. Tents back then were all made of canvas. These were waterproof as long as you never touched the inside walls or roof when it was raining. If you did, they leaked and everything got wet. These tents were made with front flaps and netting to keep the mosquitos at bay and still get some breeze.

On the end of our property was the Country Kitchen restaurant owned by Annetta Ramcke, one of the best cooks in the entire world. In the same building was the small neighborhood grocery store. To the south was the garden center, where they sold and fixed lawnmowers. Then there was the DX gas station. When we were kids we had competitions racing to the grocery store. Each contestant was required to sprint the hundred yards down the path through our orchard, make a purchase, and then try to return the fastest. We always bought something that was quick and prayed there were no other customers to spoil our time.

In the 1960s a five-stick pack of gum cost a nickel. When there were five of us and we had the necessary twenty-five cents, we bought five different flavors. Each then had a five-flavored pack of gum. At the lawnmower shop next to the store, we could buy a little five-cent bottle of Coca-Cola from the chest cooler.

The big tree was already big when Dad was born in 1918. It was a tall soft maple three feet in diameter and great for hiding behind during games of Kick the Can and Around the Moon. It stood in about the middle of the front yard, about eighty feet from the house. When it eventually came down, it was hollow. The double tree, a poplar, still stands today. It is also a giant with two separate trunks. It was ten or fifteen yards to the north of the big tree. Today it is much smaller, with all of its dead limbs removed. The tree with the big hole was a few yards north of the double tree. I don't know what type it was, but it had a shoulder-level cavity that made a great hiding place for any little kid who wanted to conceal trinkets from his siblings. In the back yard we had two apple trees and an ash tree that we used to climb near Grandma's trailer. Three or four elm trees lined the west side of the lawn alongside the driveway that headed north toward the woods.

Before leaving for the Army, Dad put in a fence post for Grandpa. During World War II, Dad served in the Aleutian Islands 1,200 miles west of the Alaskan peninsula. By the time he returned home on his first leave, three-and-a-half years later, the post had grown into a willow tree. When we were growing up, that big old willow tree was in the pasture across the drive behind our backyard. It was the same tree we cut all our switches off whenever we had a wiener roast in the back yard. Willow trees can be dangerous because the dead limbs are brittle and can break easily. When Tom was fourteen, he fell from the tree and broke his leg and arm in one fall. Part of that tree is still there today. After all the cattle were gone, toward the end of Dad and Mom's truck gardening days, Dad put in a raspberry patch west of the willow tree. The birds would eat raspberries and leave walnut seeds in their droppings. Today, there stands a walnut grove.

The first tree I ever helped plant was a sugar maple that my oldest brother, Tom, transplanted from the woods the July after his sophomore year in high school. Everyone was amazed that it ever survived. I am pretty sure the watering that was required to save it wasn't performed by Tom. The maple eventually grew to become a beautiful tree. We had a shear wind about twenty years ago that took down the old barn. The same wind took off the top of Tom's tree. After my junior year, I transplanted a soft maple and five sugar maples that came from our woods. The soft was a volunteer that came out of the raspberry patch north of the house. One of the hard maples was backed over by Chuck Hartig's pickup when he was helping us move furniture. One or two more were lost in storms. I have always loved sugar maple trees.

About twenty years ago, I brought seven maples from Dad's woods to our property. Today we still have three of these beauties adorning our yard. I always thought that if you transplanted big trees it gave them a great jump on their growth. I don't believe that anymore. All those I brought from our woods back home were more than twelve feet tall. They all took at least ten years to establish a root system, and didn't show any growth throughout all those years.

Every March, Mom was anxious to celebrate the first wiener roast of the season. Snow was still on the ground, or had just left. It was still freezing weather, accompanied by gale winds. We boys were sent out to climb the old willow tree to cut switches for cooking the hotdogs in our cement block grill. These green sticks were used because they didn't burn when you stuck them in the fire. The bad thing was the hotdog sometimes slid off the smooth sharp spear into the fire. We kids all hated these winter picnics, but our complaints were never heeded. For Mom, this was an adventure, the kind you could just never get indoors. I'm sure the real reason she liked this change of pace was that she didn't have to cook the meal, set the table, clean up, and do the dishes afterward. Often our first attempts roasting wienies ended unsuccessfully when the hotdog fell into the flame, or when the hotdog blew away along with our paper plate and chips before we reached the picnic table. Besides Mom, the only participant who enjoyed this event was Kelly, our collie dog. During these early season picnics, she always ate better than any of the rest of us.

We ate a lot of watermelons growing up. They came from Georgia and you could usually get them for a dollar apiece. We never ate them in the house; they made too much of a mess. Plus, you couldn't spit or shoot seeds indoors. We ate them on the backyard picnic table up to five times a week during summer. When you weren't home, you hoped someone would save you a slice. It would be on a plate in the refrigerator upon your return. Of course, when shopping we always dug for the biggest melon in the bin or truck to bring home. They were twenty-five to thirty pounds and usually delicious.

For years the Thomas Family Picnic was held at Brighton Dale Links, the Kenosha County golf course about five miles south of Kansasville, where Uncle Johnny Murphy was in charge of maintenance and grounds for many years. He was married to Mom's younger sister Aunt Jean. It was probably about twenty miles west and south of our farm. Their yard was spacious and could accommodate the hundred-plus people who attended. When Mark and I were in our teens, we rode our bikes to more than one of the picnics. Since John retired in the late 1980s the picnic has always been hosted at our farm.

Dad's older brother Uncle Freddy and Aunt Bonnie for many years hosted the Mueller Family picnic at their mini-farm a couple of miles south of Kansasville. This was a nice location, with plenty of room for games and a chance to explore and check out his farm animals. We also rode our bikes to this location. Here the crowds were not so big. Probably about the same time this picnic was also relocated to our farm.

Hayrides have been an important part of the Mueller Farm experience for decades, weather permitting, mainly late spring, summer, and fall. Dad's 1947 International Farmall H tractor usually pulled the wagon. Dad purchased the tractor brand new in 1948 and was the sole owner for almost seventy years. It has been overhauled and painted a pretty red numerous times.

My cousin Alan "Ungey" Karls lived most of his adult life in Ervine, California. Each summer he loved bringing his children to the farm for the Mueller family picnic. He wanted them to experience hayrides, explore the great open spaces, and enjoy Midwest food. "For my kids," Ungey said, "this trip each year was like going to Disney World."

When we were kids, we spent a lot of time at Petrifying Springs Park, known as Pet's, a mile south of our farm. University of Wisconsin-Parkside now borders Pet's to the east. That is how the University got its name. We played our fast-pitch softball league games at the diamond on the southeast corner of the park. It is less than a hundred yards from the now nationally famous Parkside cross-country course. All of our softball practices for years were at Pet's. The playground was big with huge slides and monster swings. The two concession stands served New York Cherry and Butter Pecan ice cream. These were some of the best cones I have ever eaten. Pet's golf course was in the park, so on occasion we went to go golf-ball hunting. The trails were fun. If you were lucky, you might see an albino chipmunk or the Wicked Witch's house. Pike River at Pet's is where we teenagers in May would go sucker hunting. In the spring, the suckers traveled up Pike River from Lake Michigan to spawn. Dad had an emery wheel in the pump house that we used for sharpening hoes and other tools. By grinding our old broken hockey sticks, we were able to make sucker spears. After dark we waded into the cold knee-deep water and hunted for suckers. Sometimes when shining our light, we saw fish so thick we couldn't see the bottom. You had to be careful you didn't step on them; those were the nights we could catch them with our hands.

On the north end of the park was lover's lane, a semi-circular road about a half-mile long. This had three or four parking spaces for young people to stop and enjoy the night. Just a warning: These types of places are patrolled by local deputies who, when bored, look for unsuspecting teenagers.

Mom used to take us kids to the Racine parade every Fourth of July. I don't know if Mom loved parades or just believed it was important for our maturation. As we got a little older, we didn't have to go. If we boys chose to stay home we were expected to help Dad take the sickle mower off the H and put on the cultivator. Before chemicals were used to kill weeds, it was necessary for farmers to use a cultivator to dig up the weeds. Without weeds, corn and soybeans would flourish. Putting on a cultivator didn't require much skill, but was physically demanding. If you hated mechanics as Dad and I did, it was never much fun. Mark, though, loved it.

Mom was a superb athlete when she was younger. She liked water, and late in life she and Dad used to spend February and March in Florida. On days when the weather cooperated, Mom would walk an hour in the water. It gave her great exercise without the back pain she otherwise experienced with her spinal stenosis. Growing up, Mom never learned to swim, so as an adult she paid for swim lessons. She really never learned to swim, so when she started her family, she was determined we would all learn to swim. Dad knew how to swim. With a creek running through the farm, he probably had lots of opportunities when he was growing up. For most of us kids, it was mandatory to take swim lessons for several summers. When each of us finally brought home enough passing certificates, our swim lesson requirement was lifted. I just learned recently that by the time Donna and Beth came along, swim lessons were no longer a family priority. Both girls spent a lot of time swimming at Youngs' pool

113

growing up. They probably learned enough to get back into a boat if they ever fell out.

Lessons were taught at Washington Park in Racine. It was a big circular pool, shallow around its outside. It got deeper in the middle, with an island at the very center. This was for good swimmers to dive from, and lifeguards could better watch the patrons. Of all the wonderful things Mom did for us kids in her lifetime, I consider swimming lessons one of the most important. Because of her steadfastness, we kids and later our families collectively have been able to enjoy thousands of hours in the water. To this day, I love water. I work out swimming and running in the pool more than a hundred miles each year. I enjoy lakes even more than I do the pool. Audrey is not comfortable in or near the water. She was a good athlete who never had an opportunity to learn to swim until she attended University of Wisconsin-Platteville as a physical education major. Though she learned to swim, she has never really enjoyed water. She gets nervous every time I swim too far from shore. I am going to buy a float so boaters can see me, and it will hold me up if I cramp.

When I was little, we used to go to Browne's Lake east of Burlington, about twenty miles from home. It was a trip we took several times during summer vacation. Burlington is where Mom's mother grew up. She was pretty comfortable there, and she had a lot of relatives in the area. When we got older, the lake became dirty, so we stopped taking our summer outings there. Paddock Lake was about a half hour from home on Highway 50. We used to go there for our summer swimming and picnics. Mom probably liked it because there was a hill above the beach, and she was able to keep a closer eye on us. If we ever were in danger Mom wouldn't have been able to save us, though, because she couldn't swim. We used to go to Pennoyer Park on the shore of Lake Michigan in Kenosha to swim. It had a beach with a gradual drop-off. We went out fifty yards before the water was above our heads, making our playground much bigger. I'm sure this gave Mom more comfort.

Mom never let us swim when the water conditions were dangerous. Sometimes there were monster waves on the lake, and on occasion there would be an undertow, a strong current that makes it difficult to swim back to shore. How did Mom know if there was an undertow? I always thought she was making it up. Maybe there was a phone number she called to learn how safe the swimming conditions were that day. Occasionally the newspaper had stories about people drowning in Lake Michigan. It was either boat failure or wave-watchers being swept off a pier during a storm. In Lake Michigan the water was usually ice cold, even in August.

How were we able to play or swim? The best way to keep from chickening out was to jump or dive in, then swim as hard and fast as possible until we could no longer hold our breath. This was the only way that worked to adjust to the frigid water. Those who tried just dipping their toe missed out on the fun everyone else was having. Besides swimming, we built sand castles and moats and collected shells and pieces of glass that had been worn down to look like colored stones. Burying each other with just our heads sticking out of the sand was a fun activity. The dead alewives were always fascinating to us but not for Mom. These were the trash fish that floated up onto the beach after they died.

When we became teens, the quarry was a popular place to swim. On the northwest side of town a quarry flooded and was purchased by the city of Racine and made into a public park. If you could swim, it was a great place. It was deep and about a half-mile across with a forty-foot cliff from which to jump and dive. If you jumped, it was best to wear tennis shoes so your feet wouldn't get sore when you landed. My preference was to dive. It was dangerous to be a quarter-mile from shore if you were not a strong swimmer, and the cliffs were hazardous for anyone who was not careful. Unfortunately, there were a number of drownings at the park. The cliffs were removed using dynamite. It made the park safer.

Each summer Mom would take us to the Milwaukee Zoo and the Wisconsin State Fair, both in Milwaukee. I believe they had a Family Day that made it more affordable for our big brood. The new Milwaukee Zoo and its exotic creatures were pretty amazing to farm kids, who were used to seeing only farm animals. The large state fair crowds were memorable. One summer Mark got lost.

The following year, Mom put him in a bright red-and-white striped shirt. It looked like the 1980s rugby shirts that later became so popular. Another year, Dad lost Jane at the state fair. According to Mary, that was the only time Dad ever took us to Milwaukee. The midway rides and games, animal barns, and cream puffs are what I remember about those long ago family outings.

Other memorable trips included the Hales Corners Fair, a flea market held every first Monday of the month during nice weather. Here we purchased almost anything, including pigs, a dog, chickens, tools, housewares, just anything.

When I was ten or eleven, Dad took Mom on a vacation to South Dakota to see his cousin, Monsignor Louis Miller. That was one of the few trips Mom and Dad ever took while we kids were still at home. When they returned, Dad took us kids to the Wisconsin Dells. Tom and

Mike were in high school and didn't make the trip. Imagine taking seven kids to Wisconsin's paradise, and what it must have cost. Donna and Beth were not yet born. That was back before seat belts, with eight of us in the 1960 Rambler station wagon. Mary, Ellen, and Jane once took the ferry across Lake Michigan, from Milwaukee to Ludington, Michigan, for the day.

When Mark and I were in seventh or eighth grade, Earl Thom invited Dad and us to come up for a visit to his second home near Rhinelander. We also visited one of Dad's old hired men, Al Pardington. He was a successful realtor in Rhinelander. Earl's house was deep in the woods and peaceful. I remember it being so quiet I could hear my watch ticking. It was a pretty neat trip, because when you are a family with eleven kids you don't take too many trips.

A grade-school friend, Steve Rovinski, was an only child. His grandparents lived up north. One set lived near Green Bay and the other lived on either Big or Little Round Lake near Hayward. Sometimes when his family traveled, Steve would take a friend. Mark once went with Steve and his parents to Green Bay.

Rovinskis took me to Hayward on Memorial Day weekend at the end of our eighth grade year. Eight hours back then was a long trip for a kid who had hardly been anywhere. I fell asleep shortly after we left after school and woke up just as we arrived. All I saw were pine trees and arrows with family names on them. These were to help people navigate in the wooded area. Before going to bed, we went out to the dock to bring in some walleye they had just caught. For the end of May, the weather was unseasonably warm that weekend. That far north, I'm sure the ice had just come off the lake recently. I always loved swimming, especially in lakes, so I told my host, Steve's grandfather, that I wanted to go for a swim. They thought I was nuts, but they let me try. After hitting the water, I think I came up through the same hole in the ice I dove through. It took about two seconds to leap back up onto the pier. Steve and I still had one more week of the school to complete, so that weekend we practiced studying for our finals by quizzing each other with practice tests. He wasn't too interested in learning the material. So when I quizzed him, I switched the answers around and let him see what he thought were the answers. His Mom and Dad weren't too happy when they saw the scores he was getting on his practice tests. We also golfed that weekend. I'm pretty sure Steve took at least one mulligan on every hole. We saw some of the local sights, and enjoyed being with his relatives who were our hosts.

116

Tom and Mike used to camp on weekends at Elkhart Lake, where there was a racetrack. They and their friends went to party, though, not to race.

One summer, Tim, Peter Gauchel, Chuck Hartig, and I took a weekend bicycle trip. I was in high school, and they all were ages eleven to thirteen. Mark and Kevin Young met us with tenting gear and pickup at our destination. We traveled twenty or twenty-five miles to a state park across the border in Illinois. Somehow while riding our bikes to the state park, we accidentally got on the ramp entering the interstate. I tried stopping quickly when my bike got tangled up with one of the other riders. I scraped my palms on the road, which left a scar I have to this day. We camped overnight, then put all the bikes into the back of our 1967 light blue pickup for the trip home.

In 1971, the summer between our junior and senior years, Mark, Kevin Biesack, and I took a three-day motorcycle trip to Devil's Lake in Baraboo. We rode three riders on two bikes. Mark and I owned a 175cc Kawasaki. Kevin had a 160cc Honda. This was a long trip on bikes the size of ours. Our motorcycle had a flat, and we had to wait until morning to fix it. So we spent our first night, Friday, illegally camping at the Baraboo Historic Site. By hiding our tent, gear, and motorcycles behind the big sign and bushes, we were able to go undetected all night. The next morning we discovered no one in town was able to fix the motorcycle tire. Mark and Kevin transported our wheel on Kevin's cycle to Sauk City for repair. I waited with all our stuff at our improvised campsite until they returned, which seemed like hours. The next two nights we camped at the one-of-a-kind Devil's Lake. I believe this is one of the prettiest and most unique parks in the state of Wisconsin. Eons ago, glaciers dug a deep pit that left millions of rocks littered around its perimeter. It looks as if a giant hand just dug out the lake and left all the rocks so people could experience the wonderful hiking trails. In winter, scuba diving enthusiasts dive under the ice in heated wetsuits to enjoy the clear water. On that same trip, we took our motorcycles on the ferry crossing the Wisconsin River.

Our friend Tom Carter's grandparents lived in Crandon, near Eagle River. We took eight guys in two cars in March 1972, after Mark's broken neck at Christmas. Tom's grandparents were still south for the winter. We decided to take a weekend trip to the family's cabin in the woods, a six- or seven-hour trip that had us arriving about midnight. Tom had a pair of snowshoes to help us negotiate the three to four feet of snow still on the ground covering the trail, which is closed all winter. In the dark, Tom lost all reference points by which to navigate. After two-and-a-half hours in the woods, we gave up and headed back to the cars. We hikers became so despondent we threw away all of the beer we carried in. Fortunately, the temperatures were in the thirties, so no one was going to freeze. I wanted to stop to try to build a fire. Mark was in some pain, still wearing a neck brace while recovering from the broken neck he suffered three days before Christmas. I was overruled, and a speedy trip back to the cars ensued. We had our trail to follow going back. It was still difficult because each time we stepped off the track left by the snowshoes we sank to our waists. Upon reaching the cars, our ensuing trip to Grandma and Grandpa's was thirty minutes. We arrived in Crandon about 5 a.m. and we all slept in to gather strength for that next night checking out the nightlife of Eagle River.

Early each summer we had a handful of tulips bloom on the southeast corner of our woods. Dad thought that at one time someone had dumped yard waste in that spot which produced this beautiful annual display. To this day, tulips are still my favorite flower. We had a variety of flowers in our woods each spring. I especially remember bloodroots. They were a white flower that, when picked, stained your hands as the red liquid in the stem leaked all over. We also had Jack-in-the-Pulpit, African tulips, phlox, and trillium. On occasion we found puffball mushrooms in the woods. It was fun bringing a bouquet of some of the prettier flowers back to Mom.

Father Schmidt, the associate priest from Holy Trinity, drove our school bus. He asked Tom and Mike who was the owner of the woods. When he learned the seven acres belonged to us, he asked Dad if it would be okay to set up a camp in our woods for the Boy Scouts. Camp Mueller was established in 1957.

Dad, with the help of some other fathers, built the camp. Someone gave them a couple of old chicken coops. These were hauled on wagons from northwest Racine. Dad told about transporting them through Sturtevant, looking pretty bad, and some of the locals feared someone was going to make a house out of them. "Don't stop here," they said, "just keep moving!" Dad and a crew poured the concrete slab where the two cabins were joined in an L shape. The section to the south was the meeting room. The bigger room to the northwest was the bunkhouse and kitchen. There were four bunks, each one three beds high, for a total of twelve. The wood stove was used for both heat and cooking. The big sign at the entrance of the woods read Camp Mueller. As a little kid, I thought that sign was pretty neat. One of Dad's friends put a couple of old cars in the woods. They may have been Hudsons. I supposed that was a way to store them out of sight. It is too bad that after a time somebody shot out all the windows, turning these antiques into junk. When Holy Trinity's troop had the cabin in the woods, the Boy Scouts hosted an Easter egg hunt. I remember they had prizes for certain eggs. The following October we found some of the eggs while pheasant hunting in the woods.

Each patrol built its own campsite away from the other three or four patrols. Areas were cleared where tents could be pitched and a campfire built. We pre-middle-school-aged kids used the same places when we camped in the woods. Even after years unattended, each site had some underbrush but no trees in the area.

We used to sleep outside a lot in the summer months. We were free from school for three months and it was usually cooler than sleeping inside, back before air conditioning. Once Mark, Kevin Young, Frank Penza and I decided we were going to rough it in the woods for a few days and live off the land. It was summer so our garden was bountiful, but we thought we should also have some meat. For our entrée we selected a pretty brown-and-yellow speckled rooster from our barnyard. To make this wilderness experience more authentic we decided we had to shoot our supper rather than just chopping off his head, the way you normally start. Never having shot a chicken before, we didn't know how to keep him from escaping. We tied the chicken to a tree in the woods, then Kevin shot him. After butchering our entrée, we cooked him over an open fire. When we finally thought our supper was ready, we discovered our meal contained shotgun BBs and he wasn't fully cooked. Have you ever eaten raw chicken? It was pretty disheartening for these young survivalists. Though we camped in the woods, we ate the rest of our meals that weekend in the house.

When we were kids, Dad and Mom owned six acres across the road. On the back end was a half-acre of woods. When we were not yet teens, we hauled over a bunch of lumber and twine and built a tree fort. It was much different from the houses they build in the trees today. This was a six-foot square platform we perched on tree limbs about ten feet off the ground. We didn't learn much about building, but it was a neat place to hang out.

When Mark and I were freshmen in high school, we bought an old trailer cheap from Donny Jensen, our neighbor to the south. It originally came from the Ingrouilles, another neighbor a half-mile south on Highway 31. Donny was out of high school, and his parents were probably tired of his drinking parties. We had a quarter of a mile to transport the trailer, up the lane, then by our barn and house north up the drive to our woods. After fixing the tires, we tried to move the trailer with our H tractor after a rain.

We were too impatient to wait. So of course we buried both tractor and trailer in the mud. When we finally got it to the woods, we had a great place for our friends and us to sleep and hang out. Then from somewhere we got a second trailer to go with the first, but that one never got much use.

We left Holy Trinity parish in 1962, ending the use of the cabin by Holy Trinity's Boy Scouts. The cabin then went unused until 1970. After using our trailer for a year we got the bright idea, Why not fix the cabin? Mark and I and some friends fixed it up that spring. We repaired the roof and fixed the doors and windows to keep out vandals. Kevin supplied us with an oil stove his folks had, and it worked great. Someone broke in and stole the stove. We put up another, but didn't have the stovepipe properly secured. On Thanksgiving Day we had been working on the cabin. When we left we shut off the stove. The pipe on the outside must have fallen off and sparks ignited the fake brick tar siding. During supper we saw a light coming from the cabin. We rushed down and discovered the east wall by the stove was in flames. Our extinguisher had been shot full of holes and was useless. We tried beating the flames with wet blankets but the tar siding made it impossible to extinguish. When we realized there was no saving the cabin we raked back the foot of leaves from the building to keep them from igniting. Thankfully, it was a wet drizzly night. I believe that is the only reason our seven-acre woods was spared. By the time the fire department arrived, there was no saving the cabin. Dad told them to just let it burn to the ground. There would be less to clean up afterward. Plus, the driveway was wet and might have been hard to navigate anyway. The flames and heat were one of the scariest things I have ever witnessed. A neighbor later said it appeared the flames were twice the height of the woods.

The Pike River Creek runs through our family's farm. It meanders for many miles before it eventually drains into Lake Michigan. It goes through Pet's a mile to our south, then on through countless farms on its way to Lake Michigan. Using the highway, it is only a five-mile trip to the Lake. Swimming in the creek was off limits. It was so polluted back then that it didn't even have any live minnows. It was dangerous only after heavy rains when the current became a flood. Mom may also have feared some of our friends weren't good enough swimmers. Some people called the gray film that floated on top "Wax Dale gray." Years later it was discovered the nearby Johnson Wax plant wasn't the culprit, but rather the hundreds of sewers that drained into the creek before it reached our place. Though forbidden, the creek was one of our favorite playgrounds. There was nothing we could do that would upset Mom more than when we would come back up to the house and she could see we were all wet. Mike and his buddies, probably in middle school, once found a mattress in the KR ditch near the bridge where the creek entered our property. The boys attempted to float downstream using the mattress as a raft. After a short distance it began to sink and so ended that adventure. The trip down the creek was short, but to me, a ten-year-old, it was a pretty neat trick.

One time, Mike and his buddies turned off the electric fence before walking the quarter mile to the creek. While they were playing in the stream, someone turned the fence back on. One of Mike's friends, now soaking wet, grabbed the hot wire. The shock is like someone hitting you in the head with a hammer. You probably wonder how I know that. Another time one of Mike's friends, a city boy, peed on the electric fence. That also ended badly. We used to shoot targets as they floated down the creek, first with BB guns, then pellet guns, then when old enough, our .22 rifles.

Our farm bordered the Jensens' small acreage. One time during our middle school years, we were swinging over the creek after a heavy rain. Don Jensen was three years older than I. He heard us and came down to visit. It's a good thing he did. Mark was suspended from the rope swing in the middle of a torrent of water. While we were devising a plan to save his life, Mrs. Jensen hollered, "Stay away from the creek, it isn't safe." From the house she could hear us but was unable to see through the dense tree cover. We assured her we would. Eventually we were able to reach Mark with a dead tree limb and reel him in.

I'm pretty sure we shot a lot of stuff we weren't supposed to with BB guns. My brother Mike got his first rabbit with a BB gun in the cornfield. In the early 1960s, Coca Cola had a promotion with bottle caps. On the inside of every lid was a picture of one of the fifty states. There were prizes if you could collect enough of them. Mike glued a hundred caps on a sheet of cardboard. Then in his room he shot the caps off the wall with his BB gun. We also had single-shot pellet guns that were used for assorted mischief. It was eighty or ninety yards to the top of the silo. Mike had a scope on his .22 rifle that he used to shoot pigeons off the silo roof from his bedroom windowsill on days he played hooky. One time I saw Mike shoot at a wild pigeon flying by and after it flew another few seconds, it fell dead to the ground. Some of his friends were there to see it also. It wasn't safe to shoot randomly into the air back then, but luckily we had a lot more open space in the country than now. On each of the north and south walls of our barn was a square window just below the peak of

121

the barn roof and at the top of the haymow. Each window had one corner facing up in the shape of a diamond. Over time, these windows lost both glass and muntins. Pigeons used to fly in and out of the barn through those windows. Once again I witnessed Mike shooting a pigeon, this time with an arrow from below in the haymow while it roosted. As the bird tried to break free of the barn, it got stuck in the open window. The pigeon had twelve inches of arrow sticking out of both sides of its body. The arrow caught on both edges of the opening and it fell dead. Mike never really became a hunter, so for Christmas one year Mark and I got Mike's bolt-action tube-fed .22 and a semi-automatic .22 with a clip. The only things I ever shot while hunting were one pheasant and a squirrel. Beyond that, the only creatures I ever successfully bagged were blackbirds and wild pigeons we chased out of the barn and off the old silo. When we plowed and tilled the ground getting ready for spring planting, night crawlers and other worms rose to the surface of the soil. The night crawlers attracted a lot of blackbirds that were looking for a meal. Using Dad's double-barreled 12-gauge, we soon learned how far the shot carried and at what distance we could shoot our unsuspecting prey. The weather was hot. We removed our shirts and rolled them up, using them as a cushion to prevent the gun's recoil from hurting our shoulders.

On our farm, pheasant hunting was a major event of each fall. Dad's best friend, Sam Ruffalo, one of the most generous men I have ever known, and his son, Butch, loved to hunt. Sam was the brother-in-law of Dad's older brother Hank. Sometimes Francis, another of Dad's older brothers, would come and hunt with us. The first weekend of pheasant season always started at noon on a Saturday in October. On day two, Sunday hunting began as soon as the sun was up. I don't remember how long the season lasted, or if Dad ever went out after the first weekend, but every year Sam and Butch hunted as long as the season lasted. Sam worked in a foundry and was a car mechanic in his garage in the evenings and on weekends. I remember he did all the work on our cars, and back in the early 1970s, he would charge Dad five dollars an hour for his work. Dad used to give him produce from our garden. Sam especially liked sweet corn. He wouldn't come out and get his until it was long over-ripe. He loved it tough. It was ill-advised to hunt in the soybeans, because if any plants were bumped, the beans would fall to the ground and could cost a farmer a lot of money. We hunted in the woods, by the creek, in the lane, and in the corn. Because Dad was the property owner, we hunted in our own beans. The rows back then were thirty-six or forty inches apart. We didn't have any dogs with us, so as long as we were careful, we didn't knock the beans to the ground. We placed a person every three or four rows, then walked the length of the field. We had to be close enough so the birds or rabbits couldn't stay hidden. We would put one or two people at the end of the row to shoot when the game came out ahead of us walkers.

Dad used to pick corn with his international Farmall H tractor and the one-row corn picker. He used to carry his guns on the front of the tractor by the steering wheel. On the left was his 16-gauge to shoot pheasants in the air. His .22 rifle was on the right for birds that ran ahead on the ground. Dad used to say the 16-gauge was his favorite shotgun. It was a single shot that might have belonged to his brother Hank. I suppose he figured he needed only one shot, because birds flew so fast you weren't going to get a second chance anyway. His .22 rifle he bought from the Sears & Roebuck catalog when he was sixteen years old. It was bolt action with a clip. He said the first weekend he had it, he shot a thousand rounds of ammunition. In the woods, Dad was a great shot. Few people were able to hit a pheasant that flew straight up, which was required for them to clear the trees. Dad had plenty of practice growing up on the farm where he didn't have many other hobbies. Because Dad worked so much, he lost interest in hunting as he got older.

When we were little we would carry our BB guns or pellet rifles. For a young boy, it was so exciting to go out with my older brothers and the men, but I never did become a hunter. About the time I was old enough to carry a shotgun, the pheasants disappeared. Back in the early 1960s, farms started increasing in size and fences were removed to increase the number of acres farmed. Pheasant and other game fowl used to nest along fence lines. Populations decreased dramatically when nesting habitat disappeared. Once I was out with Butch across the creek on the bank, about a half-mile west of our farmstead, sitting in the grass taking a break. We must have been downwind, when a fox, rare at the time, came walking over the hill right at us. By the time Butch was able to react, the fox made his escape.

After Sam passed away, Mom and Dad would let others hunt on our land. Anyone hunting on the farm was required to park his car in our yard. That was so we would know when anyone was on our property. At those times Mom and Dad wouldn't let us kids go into the woods or creek. Any time we discovered anyone hunting without permission, that person was always asked to leave.

We grew up with Kevin Young, who as a kid was a big hunter. He and his Dad never got along very well, so he was always either at our place or out hunting. Then in high school, when snowmobiles were still pretty new, he bought two of them. Back then we had a lot of snow each winter. He spent many hours out, venturing through many farms in Somers and Mount Pleasant townships.

While in seventh or eighth grade I had the hots for Marilou, one of my classmates. Her older brother Bill had given her a cool, fluffy squirrel tail that she attached to her purse and was quite proud of. Wanting to impress her, I figured I could do just as well. Kevin was already an accomplished hunter. So with his help I shot my first squirrel. The tail started out kind of scraggly. The knife I had wasn't very sharp, so by the time I was done my present looked pretty mangy. Somehow, I had enough sense not to present it to Marilou. Looking back, it is probably a good thing that adventure didn't turn out.

Kevin Young had a neighbor, Mr. Jensen, who lived about a half mile east of him on Corbett Road. When old Mr. Jensen died, his house and barn were rented out. A family of hillbillies from up north moved in, the Bennetts — a father, mother, and grown son. Between the three, I don't think any of them had a full brain. I just recently saw an old neighbor who said, "They were CRAZY!" During hunting season, Kevin used to legally shoot rabbits and squirrels then sell them illegally to the Bennetts. They paid thirty-five cents for a rabbit, and twenty-five cents for a squirrel.

Once I was with Kevin when he had some fresh game to deliver. No one seemed to be around. We went onto the porch and knocked on the front door. We noticed a round hole about the size of a quarter in the door at eye level. Kevin looked through the opening, and saw all the BB holes from a shotgun blast on the back wall of the kitchen. We made a hasty retreat. I don't know if Kevin ever sold to them again.

If we were going to hunt rabbits, we always waited until after the first good freeze so we could be sure all the parasites in them were dead. Also, we made sure we saw the rabbit run, so we knew it was healthy. Dad once shot a rabbit that was sitting. When he brought it home to butcher, it was full of disease. It stank so terribly that Dad vomited instantly. He learned a valuable lesson that we boys were all taught growing up: Don't shoot until you see it run.

We did not have many deer in southern Wisconsin when I was a kid. I remember one summer we spotted two deer running through our hayfield. We took a picture with the camera, but it was so small you could hardly even recognize them in the photo. Many years later, Audrey's brother was driving truck not far from his home in Janesville. A semi was stopped just before dawn. John thought maybe the driver needed assistance. He told

John he was okay, but if he would wait a few minutes he could enjoy the show. Just as light was breaking, the guy opened the door and let a truck full of deer escape to their new home. I guess the DNR decided they had too many deer up north so it was time to populate the southern counties of Wisconsin.

Our senior year, Mark and I and several friends fished for smelt. We caught them in Lake Michigan from a pier in Racine. It was a warm spring Friday night. The warm weather is what makes smelt come to shore to lay their eggs. We started right after school and fished until after midnight. Using a square dip net, rope and pulley, we caught fifteen gallons of smelt. Because smelt have soft bones and no scales they are easy to prepare for a meal. You cut their head and tail off with a scissors and gut them with your index finger. Next you rinse them in clean water. Batter them and deep-fry them and they make a great meal. When Audrey first tasted smelt, though, she heartily disagreed with me.

We had a long driveway, and we used to shovel it by hand after each snowstorm. On our snow days, Dad and several of us kids spent most of the morning removing the snow. Back in the 1950s and 1960s, snowplows were both rare and expensive. Dad did, however, have an abundance of shovels, enough to put us all to work. At times like these, I believed Dad would figure out the most difficult way to complete every chore before we could proceed.

Ray Lichter's dad's farm across the road from Grandma Thomas had a good hill. When we were little, Mom would drop us off with our sleds and toboggan at the top of the hill. Then she would go visit her mother. When we got cold, we tromped to Grandma's for cookies before leaving for home. The hill was steep but not long. If the snow was good, we just had to be careful not to slide into the creek. When we got to our teens, Petrifying Springs County Park became the place to sled and toboggan.

Our first year at St. Sebastian's was the 1962-1963 school year. Mike was in eighth grade. He and four or five buddies would challenge all the little kids to king of the mountain. We, twenty younger kids, would start on the hill. Mike and his soldiers would charge the hill, throwing us all to the bottom. Mark Poplawski was Mike's biggest friend. I would wait for him to almost reach the top before I would launch myself on top of him and Mark and I would tumble together all the way to the bottom. Because everyone was so afraid of the big kids, our team never learned the strategy for winning, or we could have been the king of the mountain every time.

We used to get big drifts south of our house. The pump house, which is twelve feet square, is ten feet from the southwest corner of our house's wraparound porch. Because we have always had bridal wreath bushes here, this has been a giant snowdrift magnet. Snow would go all the way up to the peak of the pump house. Then we would build our snow forts six to eight feet deep. Snowball fights were pretty common both at home, and before and after school. As long as they weren't during the school day, it seemed adults were pretty lax about snowball fights. Like Mom, the teachers preferred to have us outside getting some exercise whenever possible. I remember cutting squares of snow from drifts and hauling them on the toboggan to build a wall for our snowball fights.

Mom was always trying to get us out of the house during Christmas vacation, snow days off school, and winter weekends. It is a good thing they didn't have wind chill back then, or she might not have let us go anytime the temperature dipped several degrees below zero.

Most of our skating was on Mert Fink's pond located on the northeast corner of highways KR and 31. This was the border of Racine and Kenosha counties. The "pond" was actually three patches of ice next to the woods, about a half-mile from our house. Mark's and my first futile attempts at skating were on hockey skates, when we were seven or eight years old. The first step to learning to skate is being able to stand. Anyone who tried but never mastered ice skating may remember the frustration of skate blades facing outward and being unable to move. That was our story until we got figure skates with ankle supports. With these, we learned to balance keeping our blades under our feet. Then we could propel ourselves forward, which enabled us to really skate. Often we would get a ride to the pond from Mom, with instructions to walk home when we got cold. The older kids had to help the younger ones lace up and tie their skates. This was a pain, because we were always pretty anxious to get out onto the ice. The older siblings were never ready to leave when the younger ones were overcome by the freezing weather. It was time to leave for home when your toes or fingers went from frozen to numb. A half-mile normally isn't too far, except that many times when we started our journey home it was almost too late.

When we did finally make it home, Mom would stick our fingers and toes in cold water to get them used to heat once again. When she did this, they really hurt. I am amazed that all eleven of us still have all our twenty digits. The big pond was great for various games, including palm-palm-pull-away, tag, roundup, and steal the flag. Before we could begin, we often had to shovel snow off the pond. On those days we shoveled a giant pie, and could skate only on the cleared-off areas. Mert's pond had cattails around the edges and our games were pretty competitive. To avoid getting caught, we sometimes ran up on shore while eating cattail fuzz from the stalks we had just mowed down. If there was snow on the pond, roundup was pretty popular. First, we would shovel the snow off the ice in a big pie shape, with eight or ten sections. The game was like tag, except that as each person got caught, he or she joined the team to catch any remaining players. Fortunately, Mert's pond was only about three feet deep. We still had to be careful when the temperatures began to rise, because we were never quite ready for skating season to end. I did see more than one person take a swim.

St. Sebastian's owned several acres of land behind the school. At the back of the property there was a big hole in the ground. It must have been about eight feet deep and covered a half-acre. It looked as if someone removed all the black dirt off the surface of the ground. In winter, water was put in the hole, which created a great pond for us to skate at recess and after school. I don't ever remember any water in that space during the rest of the year. Eventually we learned to play hockey.

As Mark and I got older, the game of hockey became our top priority. The games were usually played at either Fink's pond, but when Tom and Mike started driving we had more options and sometimes our hockey games were played at one of the three ponds at the Kremis farm.

By the time Mark and I got to seventh grade, Tom was nineteen and Mike seventeen. Mark and I were always invited to their hockey games because we were better players than many of their friends. Usually we would get picked to be on a team about halfway through the selection process. It was pretty exciting, knowing we were able to skate better than several guys five to seven years older than we were.

My younger brother Tim later played hockey on Mert's pond. By that time, they had become more sophisticated. One of the neighbors had a construction business. At the end of each day, he would use a pump to put water from underneath on top of the ice, so they would have brand new ice for their hockey game the next day. When I got to high school, Coach Welsh, my wrestling coach, told me skating was bad for my ankles. I don't think I ever played hockey again. I also never had any ankle injuries through the next twenty-one years of my wrestling competing or coaching.

When we were in high school, and later during our college winter breaks, we had some great times tobogganing and sledding at Petrifying Springs Park Golf Course. Because a lot of walking was required getting to our destination, we went for a couple of hours, usually at night when it wasn't too cold. The park had great short steep hills as well as long hills for our enjoyment. Tim was probably ten the night he broke his ankle.

Steve and Jane thought he was just being a baby whining. They made him walk the half-mile back to the car when it was time to leave.

Once when my older brother Tom was home on leave from the Army, we took him with us tobogganing. It was a dark night, and he couldn't see the sand trap we had launched him over. One second his ride was under him, the next it wasn't. It was pretty funny hearing him curse while catapulting through the air thinking we had sent him over a cliff. Years earlier there had been a toboggan slide on one of the steep hills. We used to slide down the concrete chute that remained. It made for a fun ride until one Christmas break I thought I broke my thumb just before returning to Loras College for wrestling practice. Fortunately, it wasn't broken; the severe cold is what I realized later had caused me so much pain.

Pike River ran from north to south along the west side of our farm. It was about three feet deep in the winter. Because the creek was a running stream it took days of zero temperatures before it was safe to skate on. I don't know how many winters the creek actually froze over. While Tom and Mike were still in grade school they skated from home to Grandma Thomas's on Wood Road. They expected their journey to take a couple of hours. The stream meandered through Petrifying Springs Park and beyond. With the temperature at zero, Mom got pretty nervous when her boys' frigid trip took four hours instead of two.

A few years later when Mark and I were in seventh grade, we skated the creek both directions. I wanted to skate north because the girl I had the hots for lived in the second house east of the creek on Highway 11. Mark preferred to skate south along the more scenic route. This was mainly because his girl didn't live anywhere near water.

When we successfully negotiated the windy ice two miles to Pet's, it gave me the confidence to head for Highway 11. The only person I could recruit to go with me in the cold was Tim Reindl, an eighth grade friend. He also had a crush on Marilou, the same girl I later shot a squirrel for. Just before reaching our destination, Tim fell through the ice. This forced him to head straight for home, which prevented him from freezing to death.

At the time I wasn't as loyal as I should have been. Using thirteen-year-old logic, I figured I wasn't going to be able to help him anyway. So I let him skate home alone while I continued on to Marilou's. Looking back, I realize how dangerous that two-and-a-half mile trip home was. He was thirteen years old, all alone with frozen pants and skates in subzero weather. I can't imagine a parent today letting their children be gone in that kind of weather for hours.

Left, Mark and Tom Carter camping. Right, Dan Reindl and Kevin Young. Middle, Mark and Bill on their motorcycle trip to Devil's Lake, in front of the sign they camped behind while they waited overnight for a tire to be fixed. Bottom, Mark and Bill transporting their motorcycles on the ferry.

Sister Albina Beunig, right, was in charge of attendance at St. Catherine's. Nothing got past her.

The referee gives Bill three points for this hold during a match his senior year at St. Catherine's.

Coach Welsh was Bill's favorite. His intervention right after Mark's neck injury saved Mark's life.

WRESTLING TEAM 1st Row: Randy Lauerman, Tony Beesly, Tom Rogan, Dave Gavigan, Bob Wiesner, Gary Landreman, Steve Spring, Vic Moreno. 2nd Row: Coach Knopke, Jim Wiesner, Mark Mueller, Bill Mueller, Randy Staples, Ed Wojcik, Tony Burke, Coach Jim Welsh. 3rd Row: Joe Sura, Ron Buck, Doug Andrewski, Bill Suys, Bob Seidel, Paul Sklba, Rick Ferraro.

Chapter 8: Activities

Scouting and sports gave Mark and me many opportunities to excel. We thrived under the guidance of our Scout leaders and coaches. We were competitive, stubborn, and hardworking kids. By the time we reached high school, we had already spent years challenging each other in every game and farm chore imaginable.

All of my brothers and sisters were in Scouts, first at Holy Trinity in Racine, then at St. Sebastian's in Sturtevant. Boy Scout meetings at St. Sebastian's were held in the church basement every Monday night from 7 to 8:30 p.m. throughout the school year. Girl Scout meetings were in St. Sebastian's school gym during the same time slot, making transportation easier with many families carpooling.

Mrs. Rovinski was the Girl Scout leader, with my mother her assistant for many years. Mom was always our driver. One year we picked up a couple of our friends, and Mom would get so frustrated that we had to wait every week because the one brother was never ready. Mom loved the campouts. She always took Donna and Beth when they were toddlers. The two were always a big hit, and according to Mom, "They were the easiest to raise."

Pete Villapando was our scoutmaster. He loved kids, and dedicated countless hours patiently guiding and teaching a room full of middle-school-aged boys how to become successful young men. Never once did he lose his temper or raise his voice in the three-and-a-half years I was a Scout. Pete was one of the kindest and giving people I have ever known. Two of our other troop leaders were Mr. Poplawski, with his sons Jay and Matt in the troop, and Mr. VanOfferen, whose son Bill was also a Scout. We attended St. Sebastian's Catholic School, so we never had a male teacher before high school. Besides Dad, these men were some of the first men who gave Mark and me the attention and opportunities to grow and learn. Because I was a year behind in school, I was able to join Boy Scouts when I was eleven while in fifth grade, and Mark a year later. I loved everything that Scouts offered. In Scouts we worked to earn merit badges and progress through the different levels. I don't think Pete, our leader, worried too much about our rank and progress toward merit badge accumulation. He was more interested in our enjoyment of the experience and doing well in our various competitions with other troops. Most of us kids were okay with that; we preferred running and playing to work and study. We used to march in the Memorial Day parade in Sturtevant each May. I also remember loading hundreds of pounds of paper bundles for at least one Boy Scout-sponsored paper drive.

One time our troop went up to Portage to hike along the old railroad bed. When they took the old track out, it was made into a scenic hiking trail. It was just a one-day trip that must have been pretty flat or else my memory of that adventure would have been much clearer. On a couple of occasions we hiked from Sturtevant along Pike River south to our farm at Highway KR. On one of these we found a spring-fed pool draining into the creek. It was springtime and cold, but still fun to play in. Another time, we were stopped by a local deputy. He claimed he had a report of kids out throwing rocks at cars. When we protested our innocence, we were told that if we didn't behave they would send us to the juvenile home up near Milwaukee. It must have been a slow day and the guy wanted to scare a bunch of local kids. He succeeded with me. These hikes were probably initiated by older Scouts Jay Poplawski and Bill VanOfferen, because I don't remember anyone in our class taking the initiative to establish any type of wellness program.

Each winter we had a Saturday Klondike Derby. Several area troops would compete against each other. Our troop had four or five teams (patrols). My first year, the temperature was well below zero. Our theme that day was first aid. Because I was the youngest and smallest, I was chosen to be our victim. Each patrol was required to race a big sled and victim through the snow from station to station administering various first-aid procedures. Hence began a long frigid day with me lying "frostbitten" in the snow, with my team frantically trying to save my life. Another year the snow all melted, and each team was required to drag their wheel-less rigs through the mud from station to station all over the park.

We had two Camporees each year in the spring and fall. These were out on a farm by Waterford. We camped Friday and Saturday nights. Each patrol had its own tent, with five or six kids in each. Everyone was assigned a job including wood gathering, fire maintenance, cooking, dish duty, and grounds cleanup. We were always successful at the various competitions with other troops. They included physical fitness, rope climbing, campfires, Morse code, flag signaling, and knot tying. Most of us loved camping and the adventure it provided. One year we were in a big open field. On Friday evening each troop decided where they wanted to pitch their camp. With a storm looming, I remember Mr. Poplawski insisting we not set up in the valley. That night a torrential rain and a flash flood washed out most of the sites. Only a few of us were able to complete the weekend. For most of the troops, all of their equipment got soaked, with much of it damaged.

Attending Sunday Mass was pretty important to our Scout leaders, back when skipping was considered a serious sin. Sometimes on Sunday we would have an outdoor Mass right at camp. Other times we broke camp early, so we could get back in time for church at St. Sebastian. After one rainy weekend, in our rush to return, we never thought to clean up before entering church. None of the other parishioners were overly pleased when we Scouts came in wearing our wet and dirty clothes.

During my middle school years, summer camp and softball were what I lived for. A weeklong camp up north was held at Camp Robert S. Lyle in Elcho. The camp was named after a serviceman who had died in World War ll. I was a Scout for almost four years and attended camp three times. My first trip was when I was twelve. I had never been gone from home for more than a day or two. It was a long school bus ride but fun. The cost was twenty dollars, back then quite a sum. I don't think it would have mattered what the price. Mom was a big believer in giving her children every opportunity life had to offer. Mark also came to camp my second and third year. We had a couple of Dad's World War II duffel bags for our luggage. It was pretty neat packing them with everything we needed for a week up north. At camp we worked on numerous merit badges. A couple I remember were astronomy and whittling. Most Scouts weren't into the badges much, but we sure enjoyed the adventure camp provided. Camp was special; we set up tents, cooked, cleaned, hiked, swam, shot .22s, did archery, canoed, rowed boats, and some people fished. We frequently visited the camp store. It was a good hike, but well worth it. Here we could get snacks, shirts, souvenirs, pocketknives, and moccasin-making kits. In the evenings we sat around the campfire sharing tall tales, hand-stitching our moccasins, and carving forks and spoons in an attempt to earn our whittling merit badge. One night was specially reserved for the tenderfoots to participate in their first snipe hunt. My first year I took a cane fishing pole and a coffee can full of night crawlers. After a couple of futile attempts with no bites, I chucked the pole and enjoyed all the other activities camp had to offer. By the end of the week that unused can of worms got pretty ripe. I swam the mile all three summers, my first at age twelve. I set a camp record for being the slowest swimmer to ever complete this swim. Throughout the whole swim all the adult supervisors tried to get me to quit. They weren't trying to steal my dream. Their concern was that I was going to drown. Today kids that age are swimming as fast as the world record holders of a few decades ago. We swam twice each day. The water was always frigid in the morning session. By afternoon the water was pretty inviting. Before any Scout was allowed to swim in the deep water, he was required to take a test to prove he was capable to be in water over his head. I must have been cocky, returning my second year, because I had to take the swim test twice before they let me in the deep water. How humbling.

Mosquitoes were so bad our leaders fogged the camping areas numerous times a week. Mr. Poplawski, one of our leaders, worked for Johnson Wax, so we would all be given bottles of *Off* mosquito repellent which helped keep us relatively bite-free. The exception was the one time each year we were required to sleep in a mosquito patch. On that night we would get up at 2 a.m. to study the star constellations as they moved across the night sky. This was a requirement to earn an astronomy merit badge, which few people ever attained.

Camp is where I first canoed. We went out on the water every day. This was the start of my love for canoeing and lake swimming. Fifty years later I still exercise three miles a week in the pool. Audrey gets nervous every time I take a half-mile lake swim. Each summer we did a daylong canoe trip. One year we caught several paint (mud) turtles. Using white medical tape, we numbered each and had turtle races the rest of the week. Mark and I brought ours home. Somehow one escaped from its fenced-in pen, and the other didn't survive the winter. That last year, four of us did a daylong boundary hike around the camp, through both woods and swamps. It was difficult but a very rewarding experience.

By eighth grade I was one of the leaders of our troop, though I only reached the rank of Star, which required earning five merit badges. Life rank would have been next — for that you had to have eleven badges — and Eagle rank was beyond that. Mark and I had the honor of being selected to join the Order of The Arrow. It is often referred to the National Honor Society of the Boy Scouts. The weekend we were initiated, we painted buildings at a park. We didn't speak most of the weekend. I guess it was supposed to help us reflect. I don't ever remember doing much reflecting as a middle-schooler. As members we wore a neat arrow sash across the front of our uniform. It was quite an honor. Dad had never been a Scout, so he never understood its value. He thought it was just a weekend of free labor for the Scouts. Growing up, I remember having a lot of free labor weekends at home.

For most eighth-grade boys, girls were pretty important. Unfortunately, Mark and I gave up Scouts in the spring of that year, probably a little earlier than what was prudent. If you want to learn more about that story, I'm sure some of my other siblings could share all the juicy details.

My great-grandfather, Nicholas Thomas, was a farmer who hated sports. His son George, Mom's father, was invited to try out for the Chicago Cubs about 1900, but George never knew of his long-ago opportunity until Nicholas died and his family discovered the correspondence in his belongings. Good thing Grandpa didn't get the letter, or maybe I wouldn't be here to share this story.

My mother, Marcella, at a trim five-feet, four-and-a-half inches tall, was smart, beautiful, charming — and athletic. Her sisters say Marcella, the catcher, was the best player on her softball team, the Somers Cardinals. In fact, during World War II, she traveled to Chicago to try out for the Women's Professional Softball League, later made famous in the 1992 movie classic *A League Of Their Own* starring Tom Hanks.

When their ball days were over, the Cardinals formed a card club that lasted for decades. During the fall, winter, and summer they would meet once a month and play pinochle. Each member took turns hosting. Once each year it was Mom's turn. Regardless of the month, this was when Mom, her sisters, and daughters spring-cleaned. That night was always one of the most important of the year. We kids were all sent to bed early, with instruction to STAY UPSTAIRS and BEHAVE!

Marcella's younger brother Ralph Thomas played football for the University of San Francisco. He was one of the famous '51 Dons. They were undefeated with a 9-0 record his senior year. At the conclusion of their 1951 season, the team was invited to Miami to play in the Orange Bowl. Because they were not allowed to bring their two star black players, they refused to go. For standing up for their principles, Ralph and some of his NFL teammates were featured during the halftime of the January 2, 2016, Orange Bowl after the 2015 football season. Uncle Ralph went on to play three seasons in the NFL. In 1952 he played for the Chicago Cardinals. He lost two seasons because he was a soldier in the Korean War. Then he played for the Washington Redskins in 1955 and 1956.

My first cousin Don Penza was one of Notre Dame's team captains for Frank Lahey when they won the National Championship in 1953. All seven of the Penza boys were good football players; several played in college.

In our immediate family, Jane was our best athlete. I was No. 2. According to local coaches, Jane was the best softball player in Kenosha while she was in college during the mid-1970s. If women's college sports had started ten years earlier, she would have gone to college on a full-ride scholarship. Back then, women's sports were new in both high school and college. Jane and my wife, Audrey, played several sports at University of Wisconsin-Platteville where they didn't yet have softball. The sports they did compete in were field hockey, badminton, and track. At the time they were more like high school sports. Donna and Beth were quite a bit younger so by the time they reached high school, sports were available to them. Donna played volleyball and softball, and Beth just softball.

We rode bicycles a lot as kids. They all had one speed, most with twenty-four-inch tires. There were no fancy brake controls on the handlebars. They had a manual brake that engaged when you pushed back on the pedals. Our bikes were really simple. All we really had to know to keep them running was how to fix a chain and change a tire.

Because my coordination wasn't very good, I was the first in our family who needed training wheels on his bike. Mom must have figured out that Tom and Mike weren't going to be able to run alongside holding me up for the miles it was going to require for me to learn. If we wanted to go to a friend's, softball practice at Pet's, or sometimes even to school to play softball, a bike was our transportation. It was much faster than walking.

Just to the south of our farm was the restaurant where several of us worked growing up. Attached was the small grocery. Just to the south of those were the garden center and the DX gas station.

My brother Tom played football one year. Mike played middle linebacker for three years. After his third concussion, he had to quit. One night after practice he even took a swing at a police officer. He didn't get arrested, so someone must have explained the circumstances. His senior year he broke his wrist.

My brother Mike graduated from St. Catherine's in May of 1967. He was one of the most popular kids in school. A year later when Mark and I started playing football, many freshmen were initiated by doing push-ups and sit-ups under the cold water faucets in the showers. Because many of Mike's friends were seniors, Mark and I were never harassed. I was irritated by that hazing all through high school. As a senior I would get in the face of all the jerks who enjoyed picking on the younger kids. Later, in college, that was part of the reason I never joined a fraternity; I never liked the bullying.

Mark and I played football as freshmen. I played all four years. Before high school, I had watched very little football, and didn't understand the game or its positions. Because Mom followed her brother Ralph's career, she knew a lot more about the game than I did. She knew I had pretty good speed, so on her recommendation I planned to be an offensive end. Our freshman coach, Gil Niesen, saw that I had a good work ethic and pretty good speed, and asked if I would be interested in playing running back. Because I was a green farm kid and knew nothing about football, I declined the offer. Soon after I was moved to the defensive line to play starting nose guard. The switch in position probably happened because I couldn't catch a pass and didn't learn my routes. Coach enjoyed having two big hardworking farm boys who weren't afraid of contact. For this reason, Mark and I played a lot our freshman year. It probably didn't hurt that Coach loved the fresh muskmelon we brought him from our garden. Mark didn't go out sophomore year, because he didn't like one of the coaches. My sophomore year I was moved to offensive line. I weighed 155 pounds. Though I was a hard worker, I wasn't mean enough for the line at that weight. We did have a 140-pound starting varsity center for two seasons who was an animal. I sat on the bench for two years, except for some junior varsity I got to play. When I got my physical for senior year, I weighed 150 pounds. The football program had me listed at 165. I am pretty sure I didn't gain fifteen pounds during double practice sessions that August. That year I started five of our nine games at quick (pulling) guard. That was the reward I received for my loyalty and for being such a hard worker. Ron Beyer at 205 pounds was a great lineman who played both offense and defense. Even though he got most of the playing time at quick guard and was selected All Conference Guard, I was our best 165-pound lineman.

Because we went to Catholic school we boys never had any opportunity to play school sports before high school. It was worse for the girls. Our high school didn't even offer any sports until Jane's senior year (1972-73). She was a great athlete, and captain on St. Catherine's first girls' basketball team. If girls' sports had been offered ten years earlier, she would have played Division I softball.

We grew up playing competitive fast-pitch softball for Somers. I didn't exactly start my softball career with a flourish. Uncle Johnny Murphy, whose wife, Jean, was Mom's younger sister, was my first coach. I wasn't actually playing at age seven. During practice, I was the kid in the outfield picking dandelions. During games, I was the permanent fixture on the bench rooting for my older teammates. Late that season, the outcome of one game was already determined by the last inning when I was finally called upon to sub. But I was back behind the concrete bleachers at Pet's playing hide-and-seek. Today, I can totally relate each time I see that novice out in right field chasing lightning bugs, while his frustrated father is leaning on the fence screaming, "PAY ATTENTION!"

When I was nine and Mark eight, Glen Rasmussen became our coach. He is a wonderful man who lit a fire under us, helping us to develop a love for the game. He really cared about his players and really took an interest in their lives. Rass, as his friends called him, became our teacher, encourager, and guide. For a young kid from a big family, it was exciting to have an adult other than family or classroom teachers who knew my name. Ready to learn the game of softball, we flourished under his tutelage. He coached us to work hard and to be our best. Softball is what we lived for in the summertime. We rode our bikes two miles to practices at Petrifying Springs Park, usually taking the short cut through Ingrouille's woods and Lover's Lane. Mom was our ride to most games and our biggest fan. Catcher is where I started. Because I had good speed and a strong arm, I was soon moved to center field. I don't know if I ever threw anyone out at home plate, though I tried. I did throw the ball into the backstop on occasion. So, maybe my arm wasn't as good as I thought. Mark and I eventually became pretty good players. He was in left field and I was in center. One summer our right fielder Joe couldn't hit, catch, or throw. When the opposing players spotted Joe's deficiencies they started dropping their hits just beyond our second baseman. Mark and I quickly had Joe playing on the right field line — he had to have known he was terrible — then the two of us covered the whole outfield. After high school we played both fast- and slow-pitch a couple of nights a week, one summer it was three, because we played with my cousin Denny Penza's team in Racine. He was fifteen years older than I was, and by that time was the head football coach at Tremper High School in Kenosha.

Tom and Mike played on a fast pitch team with Jack Sodaberg, the best pitcher in Kenosha County. They almost never lost a game. Their last year in teen ball, half the team was seventeen and the others were fifteen. The following year the whole team moved up to men's league. Those guys weren't too happy to be smoked by a bunch of kids, some only sixteen. After that season their team disbanded, so half of them Mike's age went back and played in the teen league one more year. Mike was a good ball player. He played slow-pitch until he was sixty. He couldn't run anymore, but when you hit a lot of home runs that isn't necessary. One year he and his grandson Prince both played on the same team.

After softball and football, Mark and I were introduced to wrestling. This became my favorite and most important sport, and I competed in both high school and college. Wrestling helped prepare me for thirteen years of coaching that followed my own days of competition.

Glen Rasmussen helped point me in the direction of health and fitness. Workouts are still part of my daily routine fifty years later. I work out eight hours each week. Glen has also been a great neighbor, and I know Mom and Dad really appreciated his visits for many years.

All eleven of us except Steve played summer fast-pitch, with varying degrees of success. Jane was undoubtedly the best. She started out playing for Jack Roeder, a bachelor in his sixties at the time. Marty, one of my first girlfriends, was the catcher on that team. Some of my Mom's younger sisters played for Jack when they were young.

Jane attended University of Wisconsin-Platteville at the same time as Mark, who was a year older than she — and with Audrey, my wife of more than forty years. In the summers, Jane traveled all over the U.S. playing amateur slow-pitch softball. Her team was sponsored by The Ace of Spades, an African-American bar in Racine. They won numerous amateur state championships. Their team had three white players; Jane was the shortstop. One summer she played more than one hundred fifty ball games. When Jane got to Platteville, she played field hockey, volleyball, and badminton, and ran track. Audrey played all but volleyball. When Audrey was in high school, she played on the boys' tennis team (no girls' team yet), girls' tennis team, volleyball, basketball, field hockey, ran track, and was on the boys' baseball team (no girls' softball yet).

My brother Mike ran track for three years. He ran the 440, hurdled, and threw discus and shot. Mark and I went out for track our first year. All of the freshmen were told if they planned on playing football in the fall they needed to play baseball or run track. The baseball team kept only a limited number of players on their roster, so that meant most of us went out for track. Mark and I became part of an eighty-member squad with way too few coaches. The freshmen received no coaching, and each night they were instructed to go run a certain route, usually four or five miles. Because we had no supervision that whole season, several of the lazy runners never did get in track shape and logged many fewer miles than they reported. Then, after all of our hard work, we were only able to run in two meets that season because we had such a large team. With no incentive to continue, Mark and I gave up track after the first year. With some coaching, I think I could have been a good middle distance runner. As a spectator today, my two favorite high school sports are wrestling and track.

Mike was a good wrestler in St. Catherine's brand new wrestling program. His junior year he was undefeated with several pins. When Dad went to watch him compete, he got beat for the first time that night. Mike broke his wrist senior year (1966-67), and the resulting three casts he wore prevented his participation in wrestling that season. One cast Mike took off too soon, another got broken off while playing hockey, both had to be replaced. Mike was a high-risk kid, and wrestling might have interfered with his social life senior year, anyway. My brother Steve wrestled his sophomore year in the 1972-73 season. He never really became a wrestler, but later he did become a lifelong runner who has run in numerous marathons. He is the only runner of our generation. Tim the following year went out for wrestling and competed two seasons. He was a starting varsity wrestler his sophomore year. He could have been a great wrestler, but chose to work at Thrifty Mac's Hardware store in Racine his last two years in high school. That was unfortunate for St. Catherine's, but good for the store. Tim was a great asset, and they taught Tim some of life's valuable problem-solving lessons that have served him well his whole life.

St. Catherine's had 1,200 students in 1968, our freshman year. By senior year our school population was down to 1,100. Forty freshmen went out for wrestling our first year. The total team number was more than sixty. Because our numbers were so big, we had to practice in two locations. These were in the basement of a big house south of school, and in a tiny old church building across the street. We alternated sites between varsity and junior varsity. Because we had so many freshmen, we each got to wrestle in a meet only a few times.

Coach Gil Niesen was our freshman football and wrestling coach. Coach knew nothing about wrestling, but was the conditioning king who got us in great shape. Coach never believed it was physically impossible to do one hundred burpees in a minute. When we didn't succeed he would have us keep trying. With each new set, the wrestlers became more exhausted, making the task even more unrealistic. The better athletes could do almost sixty in a minute. Most practices we did more than five hundred burpees. If you are not familiar with this exercise, it starts with you standing. Step 1. Put both hands on the floor in front of you. 2. Kick both legs back. 3. Pull legs back under you. 4. Stand. Sophomore year we had thirty from our class still wrestling, junior year thirteen. We were able to all practice together in the cafeteria for two seasons. Our team won the state wrestling championship sophomore year. Unfortunately for Mark and me, we didn't make the varsity starting lineup until the following season.

Coach Jim Welsh was our head varsity coach. He served St. Catherine's as a loyal and dedicated teacher and coach his whole career. With long hours, hard work, and determination, he developed a wrestling program where Mark and I could excel. We were strong, hardworking, and very competitive, probably the only two farm kids on our team. He pushed us, showing what it took to be successful. These lessons have served us throughout life. Coach Welsh was also my line coach in football. Our senior year we practiced in the third-floor gym each night after the freshman basketball team finished practice. Can you tell where the priorities were at the time? Can you imagine today's freshmen getting the prime practice time over juniors and seniors? As juniors we only had thirteen guys left from our class still wrestling. Mark and I made varsity. Mark, at 145 pounds, was a state qualifier. I wrestled at 155 pounds. I didn't win very many matches that year, unless you count all of my wrestle-offs. I had six other guys to beat at my weight and was challenged constantly. They included Frank Penza (my first cousin), and Acsie Sanders, who were both star running backs on our football team. Tim Moore, Hank Turkowski, and two other guys were also at 155 pounds.

Our senior year seven wrestlers remained from the original forty. Jim Wiesner, Mark, and I were the leaders of our team. We were at 138, 145, and 155 pounds. Each day after school while waiting for the gym, our team would run twenty stairwells from first to third floor. On the nights we thought guys were dogging it, we made the whole team run ten extra; making it a total of thirty. We were always rolling and unrolling mats before and after practice. Then we carried them to the second floor and back for all of our home meets. We had two thick ropes that hung from the gym ceiling. We picked teams, then would have relay races. I always climbed without my feet, because they slowed me down too much. (I sometimes climbed the rope in our barn at home, but it was smaller and burned my hands). During my breaks I would climb to the ceiling five or six times during each practice. At one point we had both ropes next to each other. I would race up the ropes, one in each hand (no feet). Think of the liability today.

We worked hard and lost weight. Mom remembers that we didn't eat at Thanksgiving or Christmas. I have selective memory. I remember our holiday workouts, but not much about food, except that after some home meets we would go out to Bee Bee's Restaurant, owned by Gary Landreman's folks, and eat hamburgers and fries. Our holiday practices were three hours long. In the middle of practice we would take a break and play dodge ball. We called it war ball, a more fitting name for the way we played. In today's politically correct world, that name wouldn't be permitted. I remember at least once weighing in at midnight, because we didn't have school the day of the meet. Some of the underclassmen didn't understand the basics of weight cutting. One guy went home after practice half a pound over weight. The next morning, he was seven pounds over weight. He swore he hadn't eaten anything. Maybe he was a sleepwalker-eater.

Our locker room was on the second floor. One Saturday morning we came down to first floor to get around the barriers from the basketball game the night before. We once met Brutus, our school's security system. He was the ferocious Doberman that patrolled our school's hallways each night. Either Mr. Foster, our custodian, or Tim Hogan, his helper and our classmate, had not yet removed him from the building.

In fall 1971 when Mark and I were seniors, life changed forever. In October, Mom was diagnosed with breast cancer. She had a mastectomy and never believed she was going to live to be old. Two months after Mom's cancer diagnosis, on December 21, we were wrestling Union Grove at home. Mark was stacked on his head and broke his neck in a wrestling accident. Fortunately, St. Mary's Hospital was only blocks away. Coach Welsh didn't let the mat referee move Mark until the ambulance arrived. I had the next match at 155 pounds. I wrestled an inexperienced freshman and the match ended quickly. When I got finished, Tom Oniger, our assistant coach and a friend of my brother Mike's, took me over to the hospital where Dad and I waited until well after midnight.

I wrestled eight years in high school and college. I coached thirteen years, and have been a fan for twenty-five more. I have seen tens of thousands of wrestling matches. Mark's is the only serious neck injury I have ever witnessed.

After the night of Mark's injury, I dropped to 145 pounds. Doug Andrewski moved to 155. We got third place at the Milwaukee Catholic Conference Tournament. We were champions at 138, 145, and 155. Being excited, we took our trophy to the hospital to show Mark. The nurses thought we made too much noise and kicked everybody out of his room.

One of our wrestling referees was a coach at Waukesha Memorial High School, also a member of the Milwaukee Catholic Conference. His wrestlers collected money and wanted to know if there was anything Mark needed. At St. Catherine's you had to earn two letters before you were allowed to wear a letter jacket to school. The Memorial wrestlers bought a letter jacket and presented it to Mark in his hospital room. At the time, the twenty-eight-dollar cost of the letter jacket was a lot of money. I always thought their generosity was pretty special.

Later we learned that Mark would have died had he been rolled off the mat. Mom, Jane, Mary, and Ellen spent long hours every day at Mark's bedside. With two surgeries, two months of terrific hospital care, and countless hours of physical therapy, he walked out of the hospital. The doctors and nurses told us it was a miracle that Mark ever recovered.

Mark, and my Dad part-time, became partners in a lumber and firewood business for thirty years. In 2000, Mark and his wife, Barbara, built their home next to Mom and Dad. They are the ones my parents have depended on most. Mom and Dad were always so grateful to Coach Welsh for saving Mark's life that December night in 1971.

Because Dad was always working, he didn't get to see us compete in sports much when we were growing up. The first wrestling meet he ever attended he witnessed Mike lose his first match of his junior year. Six years later, he was there for Mark's accident. Dad thought he was jinxed. One time he and Mom came to Dubuque for a visit when I was teaching and coaching at St. Anthony's. During our wrestling meet that night, he sat in the bleachers and watched the wall while visiting with Audrey and Mom.

The following is an article written by my sister Jane, that was published by *Scholastic Wrestling News* the following December 1972.

Love at Christmas?
Dec. 14, 1972 – SCHOLASTIC WRESTLING NEWS
By Jane Mueller
St. Catherine High School
Racine, Wisconsin

Christmas was less than a week away. The atmosphere was tense. Shoppers were oblivious of the needs surrounding them. The immediate concern of everyone was money and presents – presents which are often unappreciated and remain unthanked. Apparently people are quite self-centered and greedy at Christmas time. It seemed to me that this had become an American Yuletide tradition.

All too soon the contrary became obvious. "Tragedy brings people closer together," they say. It took a family tragedy before I realized the love which surrounded me. It took a Christmastide tragedy to show me the spirit of good will among my fellowmen.

On December 21, 1971, I was babysitting at a neighbor's when the phone rang. It was about 10:30 p.m. I considered the call "just another one" for my neighbor. Then I heard my seven-year-old sister's voice. Why would she place a call at bedtime? Her voice told me something had gone wrong at home. I tried to comprehend what she was saying, but she talked too nervously for me to get the message. She said something about brother Mark. He was hurt. The harder she tried to relate, the more confused I became. I asked to speak to mother.

My Mom's voice was inaudible at first. It was choked with tears. I thought I heard a sob. Something terrible had happened. But what? Finally mother told me Dad had phoned from Saint Mary's Hospital. Mark had suffered a broken neck in the wrestling match. He would live. Yes, he was paralyzed. The doctor, however, was optimistic about his complete recovery. I hung up the receiver. Poor Mark! Poor Mom and Dad! Somewhere I had heard that a broken neck is fatal. Either total paralysis or death results from such an accident. Consequently, my fears spilled over in tears. I waited for further information. None came.

It was 1:00 a.m. when I arrived home from babysitting. My parents had already retired for the night. Sleep did not come easy for them that night. Their report to me was brief. Mark was in traction. I could visit him after school. I went to bed. A long night followed a longer day.

Everyone in school expressed his grief and inquired about Mark. I was too deeply grieved to detect the sincerity of their concern. It seemed faked. I hated everyone who inquired about my brother. Why must everything always happen to our family?

After school I visited Mark. Several doctors and nurses were in his room. He was confined to a Circo-O-Electro bed that rotated him from back to stomach by remote control, whenever it was necessary. In his head he had tongs to which 50-pound weights were attached. These kept his head and neck immovable. His shaven head was blood-stained from the drilling which was necessary to insert the tongs. Mark was very pale and extremely weak. He could, however, move his fingers and toes. His words were hardly audible. I could not bear to see my brother in this miserable condition. I left the room. My two older sisters consoled me.

My sisters Mary and Ellen were both students at St. Norbert College in DePere, Wisconsin — Mary a junior and Ellen a sophomore. They were on their Christmas vacation with the family. My brothers Bill and Mark were seniors at Saint Catherine High. I was a junior and Steve a freshman in the same school. I also have a 24-year-old brother Tom who was finishing a hitch in the Army, and a 22-year-old brother who was visiting from Florida. Our family also includes Tim, a seventh grader; Donna, a second grader; and Beth, the 5-year-old. This adds up to a big family — eleven kids plus Mom and Dad.

Mark's condition remained stable. In less than a week he would have a neck fusion. His classmates, teachers, and coaches visited him. His spirits soared. His strength returned. He was looking much better. He could smile again.

Christmas Eve arrived with its surprises both delightful and terrifying. One of Mark's friends, dressed as Santa, delighted Mark with a Christmas tree and presents. My baby sister's presence made the day complete. We left Mark in a gay mood at 9:30 to attend Midnight Mass. I went to bed that night with the conviction that in spite of Mark's accident, this Christmas was the happiest one in our lives. The loving concern of our family and friends made it so. I slept well, but not for long. The phone rang. It was a call from the hospital. Mark had taken a turn for the worse. It was 5 a.m. Christmas Day!

My parents kept vigil at Mark's bedside. His oxygen had been faltering. The swelling in the neck was cutting off the intake. An emergency tracheotomy was performed. (It wasn't until months later that I learned that Mark had received the Sacrament of the Sick that Christmas morning.) My parents stayed with Mark throughout the day. No visitors were permitted. Mark was breathing by means of a respirator and was experiencing much discomfort and difficulty. Consequently, the machine was used intermittently. Slowly, his breathing improved. On the following day Mark needed the help of the respirator only five minutes of every hour.

Mark was never left alone during those long hours of recovery. We all took turns. One of us was with him around the clock during the next weeks. This was no burden. It was genuine joy. Mark thrived under this concern. His condition improved visibly by the day.

Originally, a frontal neck-fusion had been planned by the doctor. The tracheotomy, however, necessitated a dorsal neck-fusion. This operation was far more complicated. On January 11, 1972, Mark underwent surgery. It was successful. After the five-hour operation Mark had complete movement in his arms and legs. Much credit must also be given to the physical therapists who worked with Mark several times daily. Soon he was ready for the second operation. This was a frontal neck-fusion. Finally, he was fitted for a neck brace. With it, he became more mobile.

What shock! What joy! What mixed emotions! Mark was walking again! I remember his progress well. I had spent approximately six hours daily after school with Mark during the past seven and a half weeks. The thought that he might not recover often entered my mind. I had begun to believe it. Then one day, Mark was placed in a sitting position.

Soon this was followed by a standing position. Finally, Mark was allowed to take a few steps. Mark wore a neck brace for nearly a month. His progress was steady. Last summer he was able to play softball. He also regained the thirty-five pounds he had lost. Best of all, he matriculated into college last fall and has successfully completed the semester's work.

Last April our Parish and St. Catherine High School inaugurated a fund drive which included a dance for Mark. They raised money for some of the expensive hospital and doctor bills that my Dad's insurance did not cover. My father's construction company insurance covered a huge part of the bill (almost $38,000) but left $2,000 in unpaid bills. These bills are being paid by the Mark Mueller Fund.

After everything was calm again, we began to reminisce. We thought about our Christmas, the unwrapped presents which remained under the tree, the ominous phone calls. We thought about all the friends and neighbors who brought us comfort and goodies. We remembered that long vigil which Mom and Dad kept at Mark's beside that Christmas Day. Suddenly Mother interrupted by saying: "This was the worst Christmas we ever had!" My sister replied, "Mom, how could it have been?"

This changed the pace of our thinking. We began to realize that it really was the b-e-s-t Christmas ever. Mark was alive and well. We owed that to the love and support that he encountered. We owed gratitude to so many people. We were thankful to Mark's special physicians, to the crew on third floor-south, to the X-Ray technicians, to the inhalation and physical therapists. We owed gratitude to Coach Jim Welsh, who saved Mark's life by the proper handling of the accident in its initial stages. We also felt grateful to all who prayed and visited Mark and sent him cards. These include priests, Sisters, teachers, friends, students, relatives and neighbors. We owe much gratitude to Mark's girlfriend, Cheryl, for her encouragement during those dark hours. It is indescribable the love and concern we experienced. It was at those times that I fully realized that people do care. People really think of others at Christmastime. I am convinced there is love at Christmas.

—Article courtesy of Coach Jim Welsh

After Mark's injury, Jim Wiesner and I were the only two seniors left wrestling varsity. Two guys got beat out by underclassmen. Gary Landreman was hurt, and our big guy was a pansy who pretended to be so he wouldn't have to practice. That season I had twenty-three wins, and I beat a state champion. Even after Mark's accident, my dream still was to wrestle in college.

At the end of each season, Coach Welsh hosted a spaghetti supper at his home for the varsity wrestlers. If the supper was right after the state tournament, our team ate mountains of food. When the supper was postponed a few weeks, the Welshes' food bill was cut in half because the wrestlers were done growing and back at their normal weights.

When our high school season was over, I wrestled at an open tournament in Greenfield that spring where high school wrestlers, college wrestlers, and college grads could all compete. I got fourth place. Not bad for still being in high school. I talked Jim Wiesner into going to Madison with me to wrestle in the Olympic trials. Back then, anyone could compete. I had never before seen freestyle wrestling, the style of wrestling used internationally. There was no match termination rule at the time. Today if a wrestler is ahead by 15 points, the match is over. In my first match, my opponent rolled me across the mat, and when I got to the other side I was losing 20-0. I think I lost 30-0. With the black-mark scoring system, I was eliminated before the first night's session was over. We stayed with a former teammate, Mike Rusk, that night. Jim didn't go back the next day, either.

Coach Welsh's friend Frank Matrise, who was the athletic director at St. Joseph's in Kenosha, was a Loras College graduate. On his recommendation, I checked out his alma mater. We had no transportation, so one weekend in April, Doug Andrewski and I hitchhiked from Kenosha to Dubuque and back for my college visit. I fell in love with Loras.

Two weeks before my high school graduation from St. Catherine's, I was contacted by the union hall; they wanted me to come to work immediately. Mom and Dad went to talk to my principal and explained that construction jobs were scarce. If I didn't take this one, I might not have another opportunity to make the kind of money that would allow me to attend college in the fall. Thanks to my parents, I was able to attend Loras College that fall. I went to school in the evenings and took my required finals and then graduated on schedule. My last test to take was for Coach Welsh's business class. He invited me out to his house to take it there. Eighteen had become the legal drinking age that March. When I arrived, Coach gave me a beer and we toasted to my 1972 high school graduation. Jim and his wife, Marie, and Audrey and I have remained friends for forty-five years. In the years since high school, Jim and Marie have always been so gracious when Audrey and I would come to visit.

I wrestled four more years. Upon graduation from Loras, I started teaching at St. Anthony's School in Dubuque. I have been in Iowa ever since. Who would have known that when Coach Welsh suggested I check out Loras College in Dubuque, I would live the rest of my life in Iowa. I have been here forty-five years, most of those years married to Audrey. We have a great life and a wonderful family.

Grandma Mary Mueller, left, usually had plenty of us kids to keep her company watching television in her trailer, that is, until Lawrence Welk came on. She always had store-bought sugar cookies for us to eat.

Middle left, Grandma, Mom, and Dad, Christmas 1972, are surrounded by front, Jane, Beth, Donna, Steve. Back: Tim, Bill, Mary. On Dad's left are Mark and Ellen. Tom and Mike were living away from home. Middle right, Donna with niece Rebecca and Beth sitting in the kitchen on the legendary bench made by Dad. Below is a sketch of the bench that Mueller children grew up with.

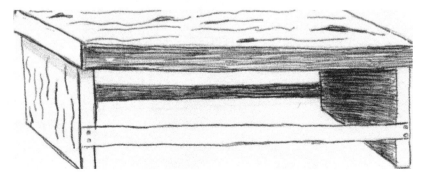

Mom and Dad in 1975.

Mom and Dad's 50th Anniversary.

Mom and Dad visiting friends.

Chapter 9: A Final Tribute to Mom and Dad

The following is an article I submitted to the *Our Wisconsin* magazine, part of which was published in their August/September 2017 issue:

My Special Wisconsin Mom

Mom has many gifts, but music isn't one of them. She had a unique method of getting us all out of bed in the morning that worked like magic when we were kids. Mom would chant upstairs, "Tooom, Miiike, Maaary, Ellllen, Biiill, Maaark, Jaaane, Steeeve, Tiiim, time to get up!" No one ever wanted to hear it a second time. This was before Donna and Beth were born.

Marcella Mueller, at 94, is a wife, Mom, Grandma, Great-Grandma, and Great-Great-Grandma to more than 100 individuals. She has the positive attitude and zest of someone half her age. She enjoys life like no other. Even before beating breast cancer in 1971, her goal was always to serve others and enjoy this wonderful journey through life.

Mom is the oldest of Grandpa Thomas's last ten children. Grandpa had four children before his first wife died. Marcella is the matriarch to her seven remaining siblings, as well as to her own offspring.

Marcella was five-feet, four-and-a-half inches tall, trim, charming, beautiful, athletic, and smart. Some say Mom was the best player, the catcher, on her softball team. In fact, she had a tryout in Chicago for the Women's Professional Softball League. This league was made famous in the 1992 movie classic, A League of Their Own, *starring Tom Hanks.*

During her four-and-a-half year wait for Dad to return from World War II, Marcella had a promising career at the Sam Lowe Publishing Company in the children's book department. She traded all that to become a farmer's wife and mother of eleven children.

Marcella and Red had the courage to stand by their convictions. They tenaciously worked and successfully put all their children through twelve years of Catholic education. Mom knew the nuns would give her kids a good education and wouldn't allow them to misbehave. All the children later went off to college.

Some ask, How were they able to do that? Along with Dad's cement finishing, factory work, and farming, Marcella was the marketing queen of their eight-acre garden and roadside stand. In addition to that, our family custom-baled hay and straw throughout Racine and Kenosha counties. Our one cow also provided milk to Mom's faithful milk customers for many years.

Sweet corn was our main garden crop. We had five acres with six to eight plantings. This meant we always had fresh corn from mid-July through Labor Day. We sold every ear as part of a baker's dozen of thirteen ears. Sometimes we were picking before sunrise. In the early 1960s we had to have the freshly picked corn to the grocery store in Racine before 7 a.m. We were paid half a cent an ear back then. On the roadside we were able to get twenty-five cents a dozen.

Marcella was the chief picker on our Wisconsin farm. The brand of corn we grew, Iowa Chief, was the best brand of sweet corn available for years. How ironic, that later I would live forty-five years, my whole adult life, in Iowa.

At a young age, we were responsible for carrying, or I should say dragging, corn in gunnysacks back to our Rambler station wagon. Mom figured the number of ears we toted depended on how big we were. The quantity increased as we aged. The older helpers eventually became assistant pickers, once they learned to feel if an ear was ripe. It was a serious sin to open an ear before picking or to pick an ear not yet ripe; neither was sellable.

Raspberries were our second most productive garden crop. With the help of mostly my sisters and several of my aunts, we were able to sell more than a thousand pints most summers. If you were too slow, or ate too many, you were banned from the patch and given other chores to do.

Mom also supervised the harvesting and sale of every bushel of tomatoes, apples, and cucumbers. We made and sold two hundred to three hundred gallons of cider many seasons. We also picked and sold hay-wagons of melons, squash, pumpkins, gourds, and Indian corn. The only time we were ever allowed to leave school early was if a frost was coming and everything had to be picked before dark. Mom was our transportation and delivered our lunches to the various hay and straw fields we were

152

working. One summer our oldest hay-baling crewmember was thirteen years old.

At a young age we were taught right from wrong. Don't bale hay on Sundays, God will get you; yet ironically, Sunday was always our best day at the stand. All of the above jobs were instrumental during our growing-up years in providing us each a great start to our education.

There were no twins in our family, and at one time there were seven of us under the age of eight. Even then, weekly summer outings were always a priority, to Brown's or Paddock Lake, Lake Michigan, the State Fair, or the Milwaukee Zoo. Swim lessons so we knew how to swim were mandatory. We played summer softball. Mom was always our biggest fan at these games, as well as at our many other sporting events once we got to high school.

Dad worked a lot, so he really didn't have the time or the temperament to teach us to drive. For the most part, Mom succeeded in teaching each of us to drive a car.

Marcella was a Girl Scout leader for years and has been an active member of St. Sebastian's Catholic Church and School in Sturtevant for most of her adult life. She belongs to a card club, and she assisted and chauffeured my Grandma Mueller until her death at age 98 in 1974. Grandma was born the year of America's 100th birthday and died less than two years short of the country's 200th birthday.

At 94 and 97, Mom and Dad are still living on the farm, where he is a devoted gardener. They are avid readers and both look forward to their 70th wedding anniversary on June 1, 2016.

Marcella is always on the run. She plays scrabble and cards each week. She hosts and attends numerous family functions, funerals and masses every month. She enjoys marathon Black Jack games running from 10 a.m. to midnight up at Keshena Casino four or five times a year. Whenever anyone visits her and Dad at their family farm between Racine and Kenosha, she insists on fixing them a meal and giving them her tender loving care. This is much to the chagrin of our family who are trying to get her to slow down.

Each holiday season Mom still hand paints five hundred Christmas cookies. She designs original Christmas and Easter cards, then mails out over a hundred copies. Marcella gives a Christmas stocking to every family and numerous Easter baskets for many of the great-grand kids. Her meals at the holidays and family picnics are legend.

Marcella's fun and sanguine temperament are contagious. She taught all of her kids how to laugh, share funny stories, play 500 and the German

153

card game Schafkopt. This is monumental. She never uses a curse word and she loves everyone, which explains the flow of visitors to their door.

In 1971 she never believed she would live to see thirty-three grandkids and thirty-five great and great-great grandkids.

Marcella and Red struggled for almost forty years, but the last twenty-five they have reaped the rewards. They have a life and legacy most anyone can only dream about.

Mom passed peacefully at home on January 11, 2017.

My Eulogy to Mom: January 21, 2017

God had a plan for Mom. After beating cancer in 1971, she spent the next forty-five years serving others and enjoying this wonderful trip through life. Today our family numbers more than one hundred.

Mom made people feel special. Raise your hand if you have ever gotten a call or a hand-written note from Mom. Everyone look around. Whenever you sat and visited with her, you were the only person in her world at that moment.

When she was young, she was a great athlete and competitor. If you ever played Sheepshead or Scrabble with her you'd understand that her desire to win never left her.

Mom's fun and sanguine temperament were contagious. Nothing was more important to Mom than family and friends. She taught all of her kids how to laugh, share funny stories, play 500, and Sheepshead. She never used a curse word, and she loved everyone, which explains the flow of visitors to her door.

People will sometimes ask, "Do you remember the order of all your brothers and sisters?" Yes, I do. It is Tom, Mike, Mary, Ellen, Bill, Mark, Jane, Steve, Tim, Donna, Beth. We all also know each other's ages and birthdays.

There were no twins in our family; and at one time there were seven of us under the age of eight. Back then, weekly summer outings were always a priority: to Brown's or Paddock Lake, Lake Michigan, the State Fair, or the Milwaukee Zoo.

I thought learning to swim for all of us was mandatory. Just this week I learned Donna and Beth never took lessons.

We all played summer softball, except Steve. Mom was always our biggest fan at these games, as well as at our many other sporting events once we got to high school.

Mom fought for her beliefs. She taught each of us kids that we were special, and we should never take a back seat to anyone.

Mom and Dad put all eleven of us kids through twelve years of Catholic Education. She said, "I knew the nuns would give you a good education and make you behave."

They accomplished that goal with Dad always working two jobs, on and off the farm. Mom was the marketing queen of our ten-acre garden. We also custom baled hay and straw.

Recently, I asked what advice could she give to others: "Don't give up, and enjoy each day."

Her hand-painted cards and preserved Christmas cookies will someday be antiques our great-grandchildren will be proud to display. Mom was my hero. She had an attitude and zest of someone half her age. She left a legacy most people could only dream about.

My Eulogy to Dad: October 28, 2017

Dad was the best role model a farm kid could ever have. He taught me three important life lessons.

1. Develop a good work ethic and be personally responsible.
2. The Golden Rule.
3. How to love your kids and grandkids.

Dad never quit before the job was done, doing whatever was necessary to provide for his family. Besides running a farm, he worked in a foundry, at American Motors, as a cement finisher, and construction laborer. For decades after retirement he ran a ten-acre garden and sold firewood.

He taught us how to milk, feed livestock, clean barns, mulch raspberries, bale hay and straw, pick rocks, do field work, and garden. Some of the crops he raised included sweet corn, raspberries, apples, melons, tomatoes, pumpkins, squash, and strawberries. We also sold cider.

We butchered chickens for Sunday dinner, along with many other farm chores. Our summer work was often rewarded with Friday night fish fries at Ken and Babe's or Harmie's.

When I started working construction to earn money for college, Dad's advice was, "Never stop moving on the job." This was important counsel for anyone who wants to achieve in life.

Dad truly practiced, "Do unto others as you would want them to do unto you." He helped anyone who arrived at our door with a meal, a bale of hay, a gallon of gasoline, help with a flat tire, or a pull from the ditch in winter.

We kids loved going with Dad to see a friend, a neighbor, or to Cox's Farm Store for farm supplies or coal. Sometimes we went with him to purchase a car, piece of farm equipment, or a new calf from Ray Lichter.

Dad provided us with a dream playground, a barn full of hay and straw. On cold winter days, Mom would shoo us out of the house. To Dad's dismay, we learned to build great forts and tunnels in the haymow.

Sunday Mass was a must. My favorite was the 5:30 a.m. Mass in Racine, which lasted fifteen minutes. Dad and Mom blessed us with twelve years of Catholic education, first at Holy Trinity, then at St. Sebastian. High school was at Saint Catherine's or Saint Joseph's. We all chased opportunity, left home, and earned a college degree.

After Dad retired, we all loved bringing our kids home, where he and Mom were so entertaining, engaging, and supportive. "The Farm" is where the grandkids learned about the importance of family. I want to be a Grandpa just like Dad, the one children can't wait to visit, always interested, and with a great story to tell.

Dad and Mom, you left a legacy most people can only dream about. Congratulations.

Dad passed peacefully at home on October 17, 2017. He was buried on his ninety-ninth birthday, October 30, 2017.

Mom and Dad, we love you, and we miss you.

And The Beat Goes On

A special happening always for Mom and Dad at a family celebration at the farm was welcoming a new baby. And there were many babies to keep the family growing. Here, Mom and Dad are introduced to great-grandson Benny.

The family gathered at the Mueller farm to celebrate Mom and Dad's 70th wedding anniversary June 1, 2016. In keeping with a longstanding family tradition, everyone enjoyed hayrides, with the tractor driven by brother Mike. A Mueller celebration always makes for good food, good fun, good family.

Made in the USA
Monee, IL
19 July 2022